People yearn for moral leadership because they want to be part of something bigger than themselves. It is a rare form of leadership in that it sees people as human *beings* rather than human *doings*, and places emphasis on what a person becomes as they perform a task more than on fulfilment of the task itself. This is more than a subtle distinction. If the building block of the team is the individual, we need to attend to the dignity and perhaps even the sanctity of the individual, more than in the past. By these means we build stronger vocations and enhance wellbeing.

Tom Frame, editor.

Moral Challenges: Vocational well-being among first responders | ed. Tom Frame

ISBN: 978-1-922449-34-4

Copyright notice

Published in 2020 by Connor Court Publishing Pty Ltd

Connor Court Publishing Pty Ltd
PO Box 7257
Redland Bay QLD 4165
sales@connorcourt.com
www.connorcourtpublishing.com.au

Printed in Australia

Cover and page layout by Graham Lindsay

Editorial credit for images used:
Ambulance photo: Matt Leane / Shutterstock.com
Fire photo: Petar B Photography / Shutterstock.com
SES Photo: PomInOz / Shutterstock.com
Australian Border Force photo: ChameleonsEye / Shutterstock.com

Connor Court Publishing

MORAL CHALLENGES:
Vocational wellbeing among first responders

TOM FRAME
editor

Contents

Disclaimer

The views expressed by contributors are their own opinions and do not necessarily represent the position of the Commonwealth of Australia, any Australian state government, the University of New South Wales, Fortem Australia or any organisation with which the contributors were or are now associated. The publication of their chapter in this book does not imply any official agreement or formal concurrence with any opinion, criticism, conclusion or recommendation attributed to them.

Contributors

GRAHAM ASHTON AM APM is the former Chief Commissioner of Victoria Police and is the Chair of Fortem Australia.

JOHN BALE is the Managing Director and Co-Founder of Fortem Australia and the co-founder and former CEO of Soldier On Australia.

ANDREW COLVIN APM OAM was the Commissioner of the Australian Federal Police from 2014 to 2019, the Inaugural Chair of the Fortem Board, and now heads the National Bushfire Recovery Agency.

MARK CROSWELLER AFSM is the founder and director of Ethical Intelligence and former head of the National Resilience Taskforce, and Director General of Emergency Management Australia.

GRANT EDWARDS is a former senior officer in the Australian Federal Police and was Australia's Strongest Man in 1999.

PROFESSOR TOM FRAME AM is Director of the Public Leadership Research Group at UNSW Canberra.

STEPHEN HAYWARD is the First Assistant Secretary, Health Services Division, for the Department of Home Affairs.

REBECCA HODGES is the Executive Director of People & Culture for Ambulance Victoria.

DR KATY KAMKAR is a clinical psychologist at the centre of Addiction and Mental Health (CAMH) and an Assistant Professor within the Department of Psychiatry at the University of Toronto.

ROB MCNEIL is the Assistant Commissioner of Regional Operations for Fire & Rescue NSW.

DR KONSTANTINOS PAPAZOGLOU is Assistant Professor in the Department of Criminal Justice at New Jersey City University (NJCU)

ANDY RHODES QPM is the Chief Constable of Lancashire Constabulary (United Kingdom) and is the service lead for the National Well Being Service Oscar Kilo.

DR JEFF THOMPSON is an Adjunct Associate Research Scientist at the Molecular Imaging and Neuropathology Research Area of the New York State Psychiatric Institute of Columbia University Irving Medical Center.

Foreword

Andrew Colvin

I joined the police force because I thought it would be fun. It was as simple as that. I was 19 and life's decisions were simple and free from the burden that experience can bring. I originally joined the Army as a 17-year old fresh out of Central Queensland and knew little about life, love or cold weather. Moving to Canberra, I met my wife who was also in the Army. Together, we made a spur of the moment decision to do something different. Policing seemed adventurous. It appealed to my sense of wanting to serve and was meaningful.

This is true of many who serve the public as members of Australia's law enforcement, national security and emergency services—the first responder community. For first responders, meaning is derived from an inherent desire to make a difference. It defines who we are. It becomes our identity. It is an identity shaped by the inherent desire to contribute to society; to do something tangible about pain and suffering; to advance the cause of justice and non-violence; and, to assist people in need who may otherwise be without hope.

First responders often talk about their job as 'service'. A desire to help others is met by an opportunity to do so. Many speak of their work as a calling or a vocation, rather than an occupation or a career; doing good is part of their personal and professional identity. Being a first responder is about much more than having a physically or mentally demanding job; it is essentially a way of life that touches every part of their lives.

It is true that the work of our first responders is extraordinary, and it is undertaken in complex and dangerous environments with a commitment, precision and scrutiny unlike many professions. It is work that comes with an inherent risk of not just physical injury but also psychological harm.

Sometimes what is happening on the inside of our first responders is hidden by the mask they wear in turning up everyday to do 'the job.'

I have seen this professionally and personally. People are complicated. We sometimes forget that our first responders are people. They face the same pressures and stresses of life that everyone faces, they just do it with a thin veneer when at work. Many of my friends in policing have succumbed to these pressures. They all suffered in different ways. For some, speaking out and being a role model was the way they coped and continued to serve. Others acknowledged their challenges but did so in a private and quiet way. There are those who continue to deny their inner struggles. They fight with themselves; they often fight with those who care for them; and, there was no standard response that I observed. What was clear, however, was the threshold they all had to cross before beginning their journey, first, to acceptance and, then, to recovery. No matter what the professional advice may have been, there is a threshold that no external influence can determine. It is deeply personal.

It is only recently that we have begun to understand the real impact of working in challenging jobs like those performed by first responders, and the responsibility borne by leaders to break down stigma and to assist first responders maintain their mental wellness or recover from moral injury. This understanding has been at the forefront of every major reform in the mental health support provided by first responder agencies. It continues to be a vital focus for people at all levels of those organisations.

The stigma associated with mental health has significant challenges in this field, making it difficult for people to be open about their struggles and seek help. The potential to lose their identity, their sense of value and belonging, is often debilitating. This is an issue for senior police and one I confronted as Australian Federal Police Commissioner. The courage shown by officers in accepting their limitations and confronting their anxieties, had to be matched by the trust and faith we showed in them to recover and to continue. This is never an easy situation to manage.

A police commissioner, for instance, has obligations to the whole community as well as an individual officer but honest and trusted conversations were always the first step. Just as members of the community function with physical, mental and moral injury every day, so, too, do first responders. Moving forward starts with honest conversations. My former colleague, Grant

Edwards, has bravely shared his experiences and perspectives in this book, and elsewhere. He has become a role model for officers who confront their struggles and continue a successful career. When he and I first discussed his injury it was his honesty, courage and willingness to seek help that convinced me I needed to react differently to what he probably expected. My concern was first for him and, then, his family, and, finally, his job. I knew he was the same person, with the same values, experience and training. I needed to know he was seeking and accepting the help on offer. He was. One of his many professional legacies has been to show that admitting a struggle is not a career limiting moment.

There are, of course, no easy options when managing these challenges. As a police leader, I saw grief and anguish first-hand. I saw the tragedy that flowed when honest conversations were avoided. I continue to see this grief and anguish in the recovery from Australia's black summer of bushfires in 2019–20. Among stories of courage and heroism, I also see the same stoic denials, deflection and black humour so often used as a first responder's shield. Volunteer firefighters, in particular, were at the forefront of the nation's response to the devastating fires. The stories of protecting neighbours' properties while their own were destroyed, injured and lost mates, and impossible choices being made, all stand as testament to the amazing work they did. There is a cost, often hidden, associated with such events and we have yet to comprehend how widespread these costs can be.

What I, and many others, learned during each of those instances is that mental health problems can be prevented, managed and the injuries can heal. Those who are enduring tough times—as many of us inevitably will experience through the course of our lives, and in particular within a first responder role—can proceed with lives and careers. In order for this to happen, we need to continue the conversations and the research, learn from one other and analyse each of our roles within this field. This is why books sharing stories of lived experiences, unveiling ground-breaking research and promoting best practice approaches in eliminating stigma, are so important.

This book is an intriguing exploration of the importance of vocational wellbeing in the context of dangerous work. There are some common themes within these chapters: the importance of listening to, and learning from, lived experiences; the expectations and burdens imposed on the first responder community; the stigma that has long been associated with speaking up about personal challenges; the hope that springs from overcoming stigma; and, conversations and innovations helping to protect those putting so much on the line. It is clear, too, that it will take creativity to strengthen the wellbeing of people whose roles involve unique challenges. While we ask them to improve their performance, we must consider enhancing our response to their needs.

The women and men who work as first responders are their organisation's greatest assets. We need to ensure their voices are heard, and their health and wellbeing remains a first-order concern. They show strength in protecting the community but they are not the super humans they are sometimes depicted as being. They are people like everyone else. They have families who worry for them, who are anxious about what they do and unsettled by the dangers they face. They are fallible and we need to protect them.

Preface

Tom Frame

*T*his collection of essays began with a conversation. John Bale, founder of the military veteran assistance organisation Soldier On, explained that he was establishing a new organisation, Fortem Australia, with a wider remit than former ADF personnel. I was immediately interested in this initiative as my research into moral injury had also started to move from armed conflict to vocational wellbeing. John was increasingly concerned with the personal and professional stresses experienced by that community of people now known as 'First Responders': those working in police, ambulance, fire brigade, emergency services and border protection. Having previously discerned a gap in the assistance being offered to military personnel who were returning from overseas deployments, he had observed a relative chasm in the care available to First Responders. Their needs were receiving much less attention, although they were just as debilitating. A collaboration between UNSW Canberra and Fortem to consider moral challenges to vocational wellbeing was the result.

The initial aims of this collaboration were two-fold. *First*, to help executives and leaders become more attentive to the moral dimensions of employment in their organisations, mitigating risk and managing disruption to both personal narratives and institutional reputations. *Second*, to assist human resources officers and direct supervisors to better manage the causes and consequences of moral challenges and ethical tensions among continuing and departing members. The overall objectives were to increase institutional loyalty, decrease workplace turbulence and enhance both return to work and formal separation processes while pooling insights and innovations from kindred organisations.

Our intention was to hold a two-day, invitation-only symposium in April 2020. The first day would concentrate on 'Concepts and Constructs' including the place of work in contemporary Australia; the rise of professionalism and the evolution of careers; identity construction and the place of values and virtues, workplace rewards and personal fulfilment; the distinctive dimensions of uniformed service; ethical risks and moral hazards in the workplace; the incidence of moral pain and moral injury; and, differentiating moral injury from emotional and physical burnout and Post Traumatic Stress Disorder (PTSD). The second day would focus on 'Practices and Procedures', eliciting the perspectives of Fortem client agencies, looking at their corporate narratives and construction of professional personas; the service ethos and distribution of non-tangible returns; organisational culture and personal identity—challenges and conflicts; what the organisation offers and what individuals expect; vocational expectations, ethics training and moral fitness; organisational leadership and dilemma mitigation; and re-setting institutional narratives and recasting personal stories.

The seminar participants were to be executive staff able to draw on their substantial experience of service within the organisation as well as their own lived knowledge of workplace stresses and strains. They would be asked to contribute informed but critical commentary on the moral and ethical dimensions of organisational culture while offering a nuanced appreciation of the employee mood and mindset. Their presentations were to canvas what belonging to the organisation meant to its members; whether and how personal and professional identities were intertwined or merged; what 'doing the right thing' morally and ethically meant to members and leaders; the influence of misconduct and mismanagement procedures on the maintenance of member well-being and organisational reputation; and, extant and emerging post-separation strategies for preserving member well-being. The symposium presentations were essentially working first drafts of the participant's contribution to this collection of essays.

As with so many activities planned for 2020, the COVID-19 pandemic forced the cancellation of the symposium. We decided to proceed directly to the production of a book. I drafted a detailed introduction and a comprehensive set of editorial guidelines which were conveyed to the presenters by video. Needless to say, bringing the presenters together for discussion and debate would have been preferable but the circumstances prohibited that kind of interaction, especially as the pandemic added to the workplace burdens carried by already busy people. The symposium presenters became chapter contributors who were asked to ensure their drafts contained constructive criticism of their own organisations. Self-awareness and self-critique are vital leadership traits and the bedrock of cultural change.

Of those agreeing to participate in the symposium, only one presenter declined to produce a chapter, citing commitment to reputation management as the reason. This was doubly disappointing given the organisation involved continues to struggle with a debilitating culture that many, within and beyond the senior leadership group, believe is caused more by moral distress than traumatic stress. Without candid willingness to admit corporate shortcomings and collective failings, many First Responders will continue to believe senior leadership is more concerned with securing praise from the political class than ensuring their well-being and that of those to whom they are committed—the Australian people.

This collection is, then, a modest first attempt to articulate an emerging challenge for senior leaders in the First Responder community. The emphasis is on personal stories because they are powerful and persuasive. We connect on a deep level with people whose experiences echo our own or those with whom we can readily empathise. We are motivated to advocacy when we realise cultural renewal is a pressing need despite the force of institutional inertia maintaining the status quo. The case for developing leaders and elevating leadership is, however, irresistible given the direct causal link between the moral quality of leadership and the strength of vocational wellbeing. Leaders and leadership matter. There is nothing new in this observation. The novelty is emphasising the force and effect of *moral* leadership on how people feel about themselves and the work they do. Moral leadership is crucial to maintaining professional standards and respecting public accountability as well as being integral to the identity of First Responders and the integrity of their service. Most First Responders see themselves as people with a vocation to which they have been called. They become their job; they absorb its persona. The contributors to this book believe that promoting and preserving vocational well-being is important not only to the institutions that keep the public safe but to the individuals who see public safety as their duty.

✶ ✶ ✶ ✶

In contrast to a single author volume, an edited collection requires the cooperation of a community of people. I am grateful for the goodwill of the contributors who submitted their draft chapters on time and graciously accepted most of my suggested changes to their text. Although my name appears on the front cover, I hope they all feel a sense of ownership of the whole volume. I also appreciate the assistance of my UNSW colleagues Professor David Lovell, Andrew Blyth, Annette Carter and Trish Burgess, my friends at Fortem Australia, John Bale and Lauren Philips, for their energy and enthusiasm, and Graham Lindsay and the publisher, Anthony Cappello at Connor Court, for their experience and expertise in typesetting the text and designing the book.

Professor Tom Frame AM
Public Leadership Research Group
UNSW Canberra
November 2020

Introduction

Tom Frame

*W*ork is an important element of modern life. For many people, it consumes a large part of most days. But why do human beings work? What need does it meet? At a mundane level we work to earn sufficient income to meet our material needs. Essentially, we are selling our abilities and aptitudes, our energies and our enthusiasms, our time and our talent, to those willing to purchase them. We use the proceeds to procure food, clothing and shelter. This is the first but not the last need that work fulfils. Nor is it an adequate account of work's many dimensions.

In the medieval period, the highly influential Augustinian monastic tradition portrayed work as a reflection of divine affirmation and the inherent nobility of one's labours. In the Reformation period, Martin Luther and John Calvin both deemed work to be a morally virtuous activity that brought spiritual satisfaction. Work was promoted as a call to serve family, friends and community. In essence, it was a vocation. In the 1700s, work was depicted as the main route to happiness and how a person acquired prudence, temperance and moderation. Benjamin Franklin offered the now famous aphorism: 'Early to bed and early to rise makes a man healthy, wealthy and wise.'

The exaltation of work needed rethinking after 1760 as the Industrial Revolution and rapid urbanisation led to demanding and repetitive factory labour and the exploitation of powerless people who needed money to survive. For the next century or more, the focus turned from redeeming work to restricting its capacity to cause physical and mental harm. The pioneering sociologist, Max Weber, thought work on a factory floor left people with an 'unprecedented inner loneliness'. Karl Marx, echoing the French philosopher

Jean-Jacques Rousseau, pointed to the alienation of workers from the creative and social rewards of their toil as a consequence of capitalist production. Later writers drew attention to the dehumanising aspects of much modern work, turning imaginative people into conformist drones whose worth was tied closely to their contribution to economic life. The notable exceptions were craftsmen and professionals. The former worked with their hands and the latter with their minds. Both were respected because they possessed specialist skills and expert knowledge. They were not mere functionaries. Their work required initiative and creativity together with the exercise of judgement and discretion.

With continuing technological development and enhanced organisational practices, labour intensive factories in the Western world gave way to mechanised production plants that reduced the need for the kind of intense physical toil that broke bodies and depleted minds. When people 'went to work' in the morning, their employment was serving a number of important personal and social needs. It encouraged discipline and nurtured devotion. Work imparted regularity and routine to each day, week, month and year. Having a job connected people with others and gave them a sense of belonging and pushed against any sense of apathy or indifference to life's challenges. Being 'at work' meant there was a clear divide between private activities and public duties, and between family and society. Having work also made leisure activities more enjoyable. Whatever workers chose to do after completing the work they needed to do, defined them as people. Further, without work there would be no holidays and no re-creation. As one trades union official lamented: 'the trouble with unemployment is that you never get a day off'. With work, life was more varied and less likely to be dull.

Business and management schools then taught a generation of executives and supervisors to make work even more palatable with team-building, professional development and social events. The aim was to quietly make people work harder and longer, obscuring the truth that work remains a fee-for-service arrangement. A veneer of care and compassion was at the vanguard of attempts, most well-meaning, to make work more than a simple monetary attraction. With the steady proliferation of ranks and levels within ever evolving hierarchical structures, and the introduction of more nuanced arrangements for pay and conditions, organisations were able to exploit the ambitions and, sometimes, the avarice of their employees, to hold out the prospect of advancement or additional income for those willing to undertake jobs that others were unwilling to perform. The promise of higher rank was the basis of a careerist culture that made 'getting on' rather than 'doing well' the organising principle for those animated less by ideals of service. It was another way of encouraging employees to embrace long hours willingly and to accept overwork knowingly.

Executives also discovered that giving a set of mundane or routine tasks an impressive sounding title afforded them a dignity they probably did not deserve. For instance, secretaries became executive assistants and compliance inspectors became quality assurance managers. The foremost task for modern management was making people feel better (meaning more content) about their jobs in a period of near full employment and at a time of rapidly increasing educational achievement. Making jobs seem more meaningful and fulfilling would help to reduce staff turnover and absenteeism. In an era where people moved more frequently between jobs or countenanced substantial changes in their working lives, employers had to make the work they offered more attractive in terms of recruitment and retention. Not surprisingly, social responsibility and business ethics became more prominent as executives realised that 'ethical work' was more enjoyable, more satisfying and, therefore, more productive. The emphasis turned to increasing the range and availability of non-material benefits and harmonising personal aspirations with professional obligations.

Thoughtful employers realised too that organisations are animated by cultures containing myths and meanings, values and virtues, and rituals and requirements. Building the right kind of organisational culture would encourage and sustain the right kind of individual conduct. Moral structures and systems, ethical procedures and protocols would allow employees to acquire an identity and find their meaning within a mindset that optimised efficiency and prioritised effectiveness. What followed was the birth of the 'caring' organisation. Through processes of horizontal and vertical integration, the caring organisation provided programs and services that made employees feel they were part of an extended family. For some, work might have been a more caring place than home. Co-workers became colleagues as social standards were applied to workplace interactions. Work became more like home in being a settled and orderly place that met many basic needs. Conversely, and in the context of family breakdown, at home there was a constant struggle with conflict and chaos as there were few rules and little structure.

But behind the warm and empathetic management façade lurked the harsh and ruthless leader who was reporting upwards and whose ultimate loyalty ran in the direction of those who had power over promotions. When not well managed, the corporate narrative proclaimed one message while the executives were propelled in another. When the workforce doubted the commitment or the integrity of the leadership, cynicism and resentment were inevitable, followed by an erosion of trust and loyalty. If members of the workforce lost their jobs because of budget cuts, forced economies or imposed efficiencies that served only to enhance the standing of executives or ministerial reputations, the affected individuals naturally felt they were disposable, obsolete or broken. The loss of livelihood was bad enough; to be deemed redundant, superfluous or excess to requirement injured self-esteem and diminished dignity.

Plainly, Western societies have gone well beyond affirming the moral value of work to depending dangerously on work as the primary construct for personal identity and the principal source of self-esteem. Increasingly, we seek from our employment what we once derived from family, friends, neighbours and religion. An individual's place in an organisation largely determines their social status and economic worth. The former emphasis on fair wages and reasonable considerations has been supplanted by a preoccupation with personal fulfilment and individual realisation. But can work deliver these things? For some people, work is a daily ordeal or a continuing humiliation as they endure disrespect and injustice from colleagues and supervisors. The perennial struggle is preserving personal dignity against the constant indignities of their employment. This struggle is acute in uniformed organisations where an individual's rank and title are openly displayed on their clothing, denoting their place and value within the workplace. It is a very public statement of achievement and inevitably it has an influence on an individual's sense of worth.

Few organisations prepare people well for the lives they will lead when their employment ends because of ill-health, age retirement or forced redundancy. Given what work means to many people, it is not surprising that they find being an ex-employee very difficult to negotiate. Without a title and a salary, a place of work and a duty statement, some people feel worthless and consider their lives pointless. How does a person construct an identity when their employment related identity is taken from them, when the work that ordered their day and the responsibilities that shaped their outlook, is over? For some, the struggle is conceived in terms of freedom *from* over-work rather than freedom *to* undertake a range of attractive activities. The realisation then comes that work is a habit that many are unable to break. Although a pension might provide adequately for the material needs of life, there is no substitute or replacement for the personal meaning attached to one's work.

This observation sums up the persona, and perhaps the plight, of those who serve the public as members of Australia's law enforcement and emergency services—the first responder community. For many first responders, work defines who they are and what is worth valuing in life. Many, if not most, first responders seek a range of non-material returns and rewards from their employment. Their membership of an organisation that serves the public interest and advances the common good is integral to their self-view and the way they approach the tasks allocated to them. For first responders, meaning is derived from an innate desire to make a difference. Work meets a heartfelt need to contribute something of value to society, to do something tangible about pain and suffering, to advance the cause of justice and non-violence, to assist people in dire need who would otherwise be without hope.

Members of the police, ambulance, firefighting and emergency organisations talk about their employment as 'service'. While they are entitled to their salary and conditions, there is an emphasis on non-material returns. A desire to help others is met by an opportunity to do so. Many talk of their work as a calling and refer to it as a vocation, rather than an occupation or a career. They are motivated by beneficence and a personal commitment to tasks that are intrinsically worthwhile. First responders believe in the moral standing of what they do and realise (and accept) their work imposes heavy moral burdens upon them. It is not just doing the right thing, but doing it the right way. Both means and ends must be moral. First responders see themselves as moral people and want (and need) others to see them as exemplars of selflessness. Doing good is part of their personal and professional identity.

In many respects, the first responder community is different to other employment groups in Western societies. Their needs are worthy of specific consideration. Hence, this collection of perspectives on vocational wellbeing and the emphasis on the moral dimensions of first responder service. Being a first responder is about much more than having a physically or mentally demanding job. It is essentially a way of life that touches every part of their being—including the moral self.

This book is divided into three parts. Part One offers a perspective from the fire and rescue, ambulance and emergency management communities. Each notes the dedication of individual members to the public and the vital importance of leadership that is able to honour the service element of the work that is done. Rob McNeill stresses the importance of managing safety risks, dealing with public expectations, relying on subordinate experience, respecting those committed to professionalism and displaying moral integrity. Rebecca Hodges highlights the importance of senior leaders demonstrating a personal commitment to the values and standards by which the whole organisation will be judged, noting the parallel importance of caring for staff and stakeholders. Mark Crosweller identifies the factors and forces that have led senior executives in some organisations to embrace a form of amoral leadership whereas the most pressing need is for heroic leadership that will not be deterred from public service.

Part Two features four perspectives from senior law enforcement officers with personal experience of the stresses and strains associated with police leadership and management. Stephen Hayward explains that many police officers need more time to deal with institutional expectations and cultural failures than with bearing witness to crime and cruelty. His insights are echoed in Grant Edwards's chapter which notes the steadily accumulating emotional burdens of dealing with situations that inevitably diminish and demean those committed to protecting an often ungrateful society from harm. Consistent with the theme of dissolving the stigma associated with acknowledging mental strain, Graham Ashton outlines his decision to 'go public' about his own inner struggles in the hope of encouraging others to recognise their need for assistance. Andy Rhodes' discussion of policing in the United Kingdom makes plain the universality of vocational stress among law enforcement agencies as he urges leaders to transcend often abstract demands for operational efficiency in order to recognise the importance of personal wellbeing to effective policing.

The contributors to Part Three offer perspectives on what has been done, and still needs to be done, in caring better for first responders. Jeff Thompson draws on his first-hand experience of the New York Police Department in offering valuable practical tools for enhancing resilience in the context of duties that are often difficult and certainly always demanding. Katy Kamkar and Konstantinos Papazoglou identify the factors known to reduce the well-being of most law enforcement officers. They look at emerging strategies that can prepare police for workplace stress and distress, including preventative measures with the potential to build greater resilience. John Bale offers an overview of recent Australian attempts to address the most pressing needs of first responders and explains the establishment of Fortem and the services it provides. In my postscript, I summarise the work on moral injury being done at UNSW Canberra before identifying the main contours of the research that is still to be undertaken if we are to have a firmer grasp of the inherently morally injurious nature of some work.

This book is exploratory and exhortatory. It is intended to prompt a conversation among first responders about the ethical dimensions of their vocation and the importance of moral wellbeing. It is important that first responders have a stable moral compass; retain a lively sense of what is right and wrong; have faith in the moral judgements of their leaders; and, return to their families at the end of a shift without being debilitated by guilt and shame. Much more could be said about the issues considered by the contributors. I am sure much more will be written about workplace stresses and strains when first responders and senior executives realise that personal wellbeing is integral to organisational performance at every level of activity. People remain the greatest asset of any organisation. This modest collection of essays draws attention to how the desire of first responders to serve the community can be protected, preserved and promoted for the good of all.

PART ONE

1 Identity and destiny as a leadership responsibility: Fire and Rescue NSW

Rob McNeil

I have spent the last 36 years in Fire and Rescue NSW. The first 13 as a firefighter, then 23 years as an officer, and the last 8 years as an Assistant Commissioner in both Regional and Metropolitan Operations. As I reflect on moral wellbeing and how a person maintains their personal identity in a large organisation, I believe both wellbeing and identity adapt and mature as experience deepens. These experiences require continual reflection to ensure an alignment to the individual's values with those of the organisation, on the one hand, and the promotion of personal health and resilience, on the other.

Being a firefighter means being prepared to help the community during all types of emergencies, regardless of social status, religious convictions, cultural preferences or political beliefs. It requires a commitment to training and readiness to engage in situations to save life and property in situations from which most people would flee. Entering the firefighting fraternity bestows on an individual the persona of the selfless hero who is prepared to risk their life to protect others. This persona comes with status. Someone becomes a firefighter and embraces a way of life. it is not just a job or career. It is a vocation with its own distinct calling.

Building on these firm foundational cultural conditions, the aspiring leaders of the fire and rescue services in New South Wales nonetheless face a number of acute personnel challenges. The service exists to help others. It requires selfless people ready to make sacrifices for the common good. The workforce is also unionised. Unions are committed to fighting management for better pay and conditions for their members. At times, the personal interests and aspirations of leaders and followers complicates, and even constrains, the organisation. Firefighters face an inner tension between their interests and the interests of those they serve. Michael Wright's 2008 doctoral thesis entitled, 'Contested Firegrounds', drew attention to long-standing struggles between volunteer firefighters, quasi-volunteer firefighters (that is, on-call retained firefighters) and career firefighters. The contest between decentralised regional volunteer fire brigades and centralist career fire brigades has produced a century-long battle for control, ensuring a strong and sometimes militant industrial arm exists to support the career firefighters. Additionally, fire services leaders usually graduate through the union ranks progressing steadily from membership to leadership positions.

The progression to leadership also entails operational experiences and the making of decisions that challenge and, at times, haunt those who have to make them. These decisions are embedded in bodies and minds. They become part of someone's identity as a firefighter. Individual bonding to the identity of being a firefighter seems to deepen and be reinforced with each community engagement and every emergency incident. Those who fight fires are part of what feels like an extended family.

Reflecting on my own journey and my time in the emergency services, I have come to recognise four clear phases in my professional life. In fact, I only became aware of the last phase while drafting this chapter. The first is the *task* phase: where you are on the truck, part of a team, living to respond to that emergency incident that will challenge and reward you and the team in the saving of life and property. The second is the *tactical* phase: you are in charge of the truck and have responsibility for the crew, the lives and property you are tasked to protect which become your single-minded focus. The third is the *strategic* phase: you are accountable for ensuring your command is prepared, capable and has capacity to ensure the safety of your firefighters and the communities assigned to you. The fourth is the *exit* phase: I cannot reflect in any great detail on this phase. But I can ponder what this phase might mean as it quickly heads towards me. I greet it with mixed emotions, swinging between the loss of identity and, therefore, my reason for being and a release from the burdens of leadership and growing regard for the earlier three phases of my career.

Realising the identity

The journey through the ranks of firefighting is a good grounding to understanding implicitly why the fire service exists. It gave me a good insight into the many reasons firefighters become firefighters and what drives them to render service to the community. I have recognised other leaders in the fire services who have not had that experience of proceeding through the ranks, missing opportunities to engage with firefighters when leading change and improving service delivery. In my judgement, the absence of this experience has left those leaders with a void. They do not properly appreciate the moral essence of why their team of firefighters comes to work each day. Not having taken a reflective journey through the phases I have identified can lead to a misalignment of leadership values between the workforce (organisation) and the leader themselves. Further, assuming leadership without having experienced the long journey that other colleagues have known has many legacies. The foremost is whether the leader possesses the four 'Cs'. Are they capable, credible, consistent and committed (J Fewtrell, 2010). The journey through the ranks ensures the development of capability and character. It builds resilience and the capacity to make the right leadership decisions both in operational and corporate settings. Let me illustrate my point with a practical example.

During the late 1990s I attended an incident at a major hospital in Sydney. It was a Thursday night—pension night—which is a notorious night for drug overdoses. Hospitals are often pushed to their limits on a Thursday night. The incident involved a chemical poisoning suicide. The victim was suspected of emitting toxic vapour in the hospital's emergency department. As we arrived at the scene, medical staff were evacuating the area. Our team gathered information from the treating doctor. Our challenge was rendering safe the emergency department, and the whole hospital for that matter, and removing the body safely. I was also conscious that time was of the essence. Other Sydney hospitals were being steadily overloaded with new cases to the extent that some patients needed to be transported long distances to other available hospitals for life saving treatment. How was I going to move this body quickly, safely and in a dignified manner to allow the hospital to reopen?

I engaged my crew. One firefighter suggested we place the deceased in one of our chemical suits and seal the valves. The person could be identified by his next of kin, moved to the mortuary and the emergency department cleaned ahead of the hospital reopening. It was a good plan. We had the first C—*Capable*. All of the resources were in place. The contractor who would move the deceased was ready. The snag was that I never engaged the contractor personally nor did I explain the plan or assure him with adequate information that he would

be safe. I did not mention allowing a Hazmat Firefighter to travel with him to the mortuary. Once we removed the deceased and had him identified by next of kin, we started to place him in the mortuary contractor's van. The contractor refused to take custody of the deceased. He was concerned for his own safety and did not want to be locked in a vehicle with this potentially toxic human bomb. I then had to look for an alternative as pressure to reopen the hospital was mounting. Out of sheer desperation, I decided to place the deceased in a Hazmat bin. It was an undignified way of handling human remains but I was committed to achieving the best outcome for the whole community.

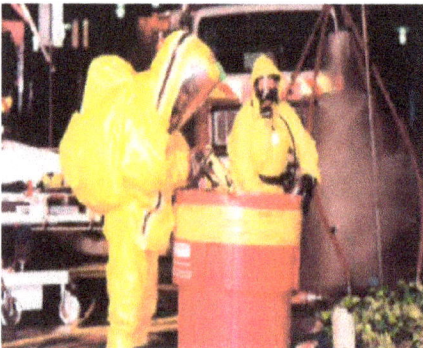

The following morning this incident received national media attention and led to much debate on the best way to manage chemical medical emergencies. My immediate reflection was that I had done the right thing. This was a source of moral comfort. Sometime later while presenting to a group of police commanders, I realised the situation could have been resolved by engaging the mortuary contractor on a personal level and ensuring his safety. Doing so was neither demanding nor difficult.

Why we did what we did was morally defensible. We needed to reopen the hospital. How I led my team could have been better. We might have achieved a more dignified outcome. Plainly, we had a safe and dignified plan for removing the deceased. The plan failed at the execution stage due to a lack of engagement and sufficient consultation with everyone in the team. I concluded was not *Capable* as I had not achieved that higher level of Emotional Intelligence (EI) that is required of a leader to ensure each person feels safe in the environments in which they work.

I realised during that presentation to police commanders following the 'body in the bin' incident, my thinking and approach to leading teams in the future had changed. I strived to ensure that everyone involved in operations or projects was engaged and aware of the details, the risks and their respective roles. The aim was creating a safe environment for people while building my resilience and increasing my ability to meet the responsibilities of making the right decision in difficult times.

The next ten years of my career included preparations for the 2000 Sydney Olympics, the 2007 APEC Australia conference, and the 2008 Catholic World Youth Day in Sydney. It also covered many other events: developing and delivering specialist capability in hazardous materials and Chemical, Biological, Radiological and Nuclear (CRBN) emergency management across many emergency services, police and allied functional areas. During this time the September 11 terrorist attacks occurred in the United States and the invasions of Afghanistan and Iraq followed. Outside these operational preparedness and response activities, I had the good fortune to lead and play major roles in projects focussed on developing capability in the areas of basic life support for firefighters, hazardous material response, counter-terrorism preparedness and response, community safety, Urban Search and Rescue and firefighting. This allowed me to construct a strong network of reliable contacts and trusted experts across many fields including emergency management, policing, hazardous materials, health and numerous other functional areas. These contacts were invaluable in supporting the decisions that I would have to make in an operational setting and in building the capabilities of the New South Wales fire service.

My professional career was challenging, exciting and rewarding. I was doing a good job managing major events and completing crucial projects. I was gaining many new skills and attributes within a network of likeminded leaders in the Emergency Management, Hazmat and CBRN world. By way of contrast, my personal life was full of turmoil. My first marriage to a woman I truly loved and with whom I had two beautiful girls had fallen apart. I rebounded into another marriage with a much-loved son and a step daughter.

Fourteen years later, this marriage also ended. To this point I managed to keep my career and home life totally separate. My second partner did not enjoy having an absent soul in the relationship.

A little more than ten years later, I was tasked with leading the Australian Urban Search and Rescue Task Force response to the devastating earthquake and tsunami impacting the east cost of Japan. We started the deployment to Japan on 12 March 2011 with a 72-person strong Urban Search and Rescue (USAR) Task Force. The Japanese earthquake and tsunami was a disaster being played out on the world stage and USAR teams from all over the world were involved. The disaster was evolving as a multi-faceted event involving structural collapse, tsunami inundation of populated areas and the failure of a major nuclear reactor at Fukushima. This produced many critical factors that needed to be managed well to ensure the success of the deployment and the well-being of all deployed personnel.

I knew we had to create a safe environment for the team from aftershocks, further tsunamis, radiation exposure and protection from the winter cold. At the pre-deployment briefing I drew on what I had learned and refined over 27 years in the fire service. I needed to be a capable, committed, consistent and credible leader for this type of challenging deployment. I briefed the 72-person team on the situation, the risks and the why we were deploying.

The *why* of our deployment was the foundation for all subsequent decision-making. At the pre-deployment briefing all commanders on the team came to the logical conclusion that there would be little chance of rescue as the collapsed buildings had been inundated by water and any trapped survivors would have perished. Hence, we identified the *why*. We were going 'to give humanitarian aid to the Japanese communities' that were affected by this disaster.

During the briefing sessions with the whole team present, we spent some time creating a physical and psychological safe environment. The team was to be fully self-sufficient in all basic needs such as shelter, food and water for up to 10 days. I worked with other agencies, such as the Australian Radiation Protection and Nuclear Safety Agency (ARPANSA), Australian Nuclear Science and Technology Organisation, Bureau of Meteorology, the New South Wales Environmental Protection Authority and other trusted experts to develop a safe operational plan for the deployment. Crews were prepared, Hazardous Materials Technicians (Hazmat) were refreshed on radiation protection management, the radiation exposure management policy and procedure were activated, and all crews were briefed.

After considerable planning to identify the most suitable military aircraft to convey our 72-person team and 20 tonnes of equipment (noting the war in Afghanistan and Australia's USAR taskforce was in Christchurch after the February 2011 earthquake), the Australian Defence Force (ADF) made available a Boeing C-17 Globemaster transport aircraft. After being delayed by 10 hours to meet CASA requirements, we finally deployed on Sunday 13 March. After a complex travel transfer, involving a New South Wales state team being deployed by the Commonwealth Government in an ADF aircraft landing on a United States military airfield at Yokota, we started our journey to the earthquake and tsunami devastated region of Tohoku to search the areas of Shizugawa, Rikuzentogura and Minamisanriku.

Our Base of Operations (BoO) was the baseball field in Tome city in the Miyagi Prefecture. It was selected to reduce the risk of aftershock and possible tsunami. Australian USAR Task Force 1 then commenced establishing BoO facilities while I met with the other three international USAR teams co-located with us at the baseball fields.

I walked into the Command tent with the three other leaders. I then noticed a flip chart depicting the east coast of Japan, the location of the Fukushima nuclear reactor and our BoO. Drawn on the map was the Japanese calculation of where the radiation plume from Fukushima was travelling. The map indicated it was flowing over our location which was 130 kilometres from the failing nuclear reactor. This information did not match the information I had received from my trusted network of experts in Australia nor did it reflect what our Hazmat team was telling me from their radiation detection equipment. We had implemented our radiation exposure management policy and procedures which were designed to assess our exposure to radiation continually. Australian media were reporting problems at the Fukushima nuclear reactor and the expanding exclusion zone, now set at 80 kilometres. The families of our team were letting them know by text how worried they were about them.

Media reports claimed that Australian USAR Task Force members were being exposed to the Fukushima radiation after a failed Black Hawk helicopter reconnaissance mission. Due to the domestic politics of nuclear power and radiation, our presence in Japan was generating angst within government agencies and among our families and friends. I met USAR leaders from the other countries. They had already come to the conclusion the area had to be evacuated. We needed to return to a safe area, believing we were all in imminent danger of lethal radiation poisoning. At this point I was confronted with the most significant operational and moral leadership decision of my career. I had the safety of 76 people, including four staff from the Department of Foreign Affairs and Trade (DFAT), in my hands, together with our commitment to delivering support and humanitarian aid to the suffering Japanese. The other USAR teams were pushing the point that if one international team leaves the area, every team needed to leave to validate the decision and preclude international embarrassment. I was also concerned that my position on the possible or actual radiation risk may not be reliable or correct.

I could not give an instantaneous 'gut' reply to the other Task Force leaders. The possible decision to leave challenged my thoughts and beliefs. It would have been easy to comply with group thinking in the short term and to depart under the perceived risk of radiation poisoning. But could I have lived with that feeling that such a decision was not the right one? My intuition, built on 'recognition primed decision making', told me to resist. My support network of subject matter experts (SME) were saying we were safe for 48 hours given the current weather conditions. The team had in place radiation safety procedures endorsed by ARPANSA and ANSTO. We had a timely escape route if conditions were to change, with support from the American and Australian militaries. I was convinced that a safe operating environment had been created for the Australian USAR Task Force. Notably, we were there to give humanitarian assistance to people in the Tohoku region after the most devastating natural disaster in Japan's modern history.

Instead of giving a quick answer to the other USAR leaders, I wanted some clear air to discuss the situation with my SMEs and my team. I left the command tent, rang my contact at ANSTO and asked him to re-confirm our position in regard to radiation risk, which he did. I then rallied the team together and informed them of the prevailing and impending situation. I asked the team members if they wanted to stay or leave. They unanimously agreed to stay, saying they had confidence in our safety arrangements and they wanted to get on with helping the Japanese people. The fears associated with making this critical decision evaporated. I walked back into the tent feeling confident we were doing things right, and doing the right thing. I informed the other USAR leaders that the Australians would be staying. They noted there would probably be few people to rescue given the voids of collapsed building had been inundated with water. Further, with temperatures hovering around -15 celsius, most of the initial survivors would probably have perished by now. I affirmed that rescuing people was not the main reason we were in Japan. We knew that surviving the earthquake and tsunami would be nearly impossible. We were there, however, to walk with Japanese emergency services personnel through this disaster and to help their fellow citizens. I recognised that the firefighting family is worldwide and that a shared identity becomes a deep seated personal trait. Notwithstanding my decision, one team evacuated immediately. Two of the other teams stayed for a couple of days and then left.

The decision to stay was a complex leadership decision made rapidly and delivered to the team leaders within 30 minutes. The decision was made principally in the interests of team safety, conscious of the moral basis for our deployment and mindful of the capability of our team and support networks. Making the decision to remain resulted in Australian USAR personnel returning to their careers and families with a feeling of achievement. They had fulfilled a career aspiration, knowing they had done the right thing by the Japanese people. They were also confident they had not been exposed to excessive radiation and been the cause of continuing concern for the governments that deployed them.

On returning to Australia at the end of our mission, my mind returned to the late 1990s when I visited my grandfather in hospital. He was then in his 80s. He served in the Second Australian Imperial Force in the Second World War. In 1945 he fought the Japanese at Labuan in Borneo. I visited him in uniform at Liverpool Hospital. He was delirious and wired up to a number of medical machines. He looked up at me before grabbing me from his bed and pulling me down to his chest in a head lock. He was obviously experiencing a flash back to the war. I said to him: ' Pop, it is me, Robert'. He replied: 'well get down here with me before you get killed'. Pop passed away in 2004. He was 95 years old. I thought of how far we have come in 66 years. The Japanese had moved from being our foes to becoming our friends. My recent experience had shown me how two countries had put aside the horrors of war and went to extraordinary lengths to help each other. The decision to stay and help during a moment of intense personal risk, while reflecting on my grandfather's experiences, made me feel the right message was being sent by both countries. It was a timely message given the conflicts that were besetting other parts of the world: in Libya, Syria, Afghanistan and Iraq.

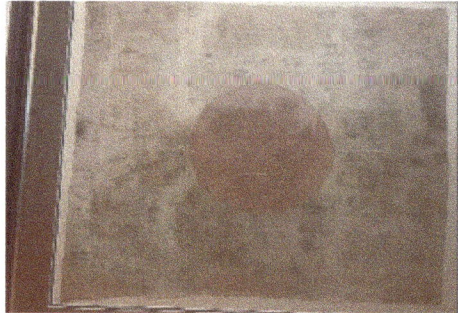

I entered the next phase of my career in 2012. I was successful in gaining the position of Assistant Commissioner, Regional Operations and accepted the strategic role of ensuring safety, capability and community resilience in Regional New South Wales. My first challenge was working with unions, government and the workforce to create a new 'On Call Retained Firefighter Award', noting that for On-Call firefighters, firefighting is not their primary employment. On-Call firefighters are contacted by pager or text message. They are obliged to leave their daily routine and respond to emergency incidents in their home town, at any time day or night, every day of the year. The challenges in this phase were complicated by what I knew of the task and tactical phases. As I moved through these phases I had benefited from the contributions of the union, ensuring working conditions were continually improved and adequate remuneration was maintained. I felt a continuing personal debt to the union and an abiding commitment to its charter.

Most career firefighters are loyal to their union. They are also aware that the inherently dangerous nature of the job has earned all firefighters an exalted position in the communities they serve. Career, semi-volunteer (On Call) and volunteer firefighters do the same job and face the same challenges. The majority of the firefighters I lead are On Call Retained Firefighters. An effective On Call Retained Firefighter movement negates the need for an increase in Career Permanent firefighters across regional New South Wales. There is an unspoken divide between the two groups, both delivering the same service to the community.

On Call and Career firefighters identity as firefighters. It is a big part of who they are albeit in different contexts. They both protect life and property. The On Call firefighter is focused mainly on the local community. Most are usually local leaders in other capacities. The Career firefighter is more vocation than community oriented. He or she serves the state and its interests. I have developed a deep loyalty to the cause of On Call firefighters and the selfless passion and commitment they display in serving their community. To that end, I worked with the industrial relations team and the Fire Brigades' Union for eight months developing an industrial award for On Call Retained Firefighters. The foremost principle was paying them to be available and ready to respond to emergency incidents. The previous focus of remuneration was paying them for the number of incidents they attended; overlooked was the fact that they were available as a stand-alone brigade that was on call at every moment of every day. I was drawn to the obvious inequities between the two groups. The employment benefits enjoyed by Career firefighters were far superior although both groups delivered the same service.

While developing the award I was working on narrowing the inequity between the two groups within a tightly defined budget. We had developed an availability system with increasing pay increments for increased levels of availability. Effectively, this system would change the readiness and response model from calling out all On Call Retained Firefighters to each emergency incident to one of grouping On Call firefighters at each station into platoons to spread the load of availability requirements. The model was nearly ready to be launched when a group of 20 station captains heard about the proposal. They were unhappy, believing it posed a major risk to the future viability of the On Call Retained firefighter system. This meant it would have a direct impact on their primary employment. The group of station captains from the northern region of New South Wales invited me to attend a social weekend at Port Macquarie so they could discuss the proposed new system of work we were designing for them. I accepted the invitation knowing they did not support the concept. I thought of all the ways I could convince them that it was the best system for them. Initially, I felt as though I had no choice. I could not waste eight months of work. It was, I was persuaded, the best way to ensure the On Call Retained system survived. Of course, it would not reflect well on my performance if I failed to produce a result after eight months of negotiations with the union.

When I arrived at the North Coast station captains' lunch, they sat me down and told me clearly the idea was doomed to fail. They explained that the critical point of failure was that I did not understand the depth and breadth of On Call firefighter availability. Due to varying levels of primary employment flexibility, some On Call firefighters were 100 percent available, some 50 percent and some 10 percent. Their availability depended on the severity of the emergency call and what they were specifically doing at the time. I listened and understood. I was confronted with what I had observed. It was another career defining decision. The right thing was to accept their advice and realign the award negotiations to meet their needs. After all, they were the people that made the whole service work. But I also had to front the Commissioner, informing him that we had to go back to the negotiating table and abandon an availability management scheme that was based on a platoon system for On Call Retained firefighters.

It took three hours of driving before I mustered the courage to call the Commissioner. It proved to be an easy, sensible conversation resulting in agreement. We would rebuild the award to suit the station captains' needs. Once I had the agreement of the Commissioner, I thought how fortunate I was that the station captains felt sufficiently secure to explain the faults in the proposal. They offered ideas on how a revised proposal could be made to work and offered their support for a new system of work incorporating the matters we discussed. The station captains believed the new award could threaten their capacity to function as On Call firefighters. This role was very important to them personally. It shaped their identity in their community. They were the protectors of their communities and were held in high regard.

Although the 2014 'Retained Firefighters Award' did not greatly reduce the inequities between On Call Retained Firefighters and On Duty Career Firefighters, the world was not turned upside down. These firefighters continue to serve the community. There is a continuing movement within Fire and Rescue NSW to better appreciate the value of On Call Retained firefighters and a commitment to making structural changes in conditions and facilities to support the service they provide. As I reflect on the key factors associated with these decisions, I recognise they were based on achieving the best community outcome including the safety of firefighters. I concluded that my moral beliefs were aligned with those of the organisation and no personal or professional compromise was needed.

Developing a high-level capability across all aspects of emergency services work, gaining credibility among the personnel who deliver the tactical components of that service and applying a consistent personal moral standard to decisions are not incompatible or inconsistent objectives. Once the right balance between personal aspirations and corporate priorities is achieved, and the workforce needs to be an active participant in this process, an organisation and its members can be confident that the right decision will be made.

I suggested there are four phases in a firefighter's career. I am about to enter the fourth phase—retirement. It marks a significant change for a firefighter. It is a moment of walking away. In looking forward to the retirement phase, I wonder if I had acquired and applied the same level of capability in my personal relationships, if I had shown a greater commitment to my other occupations and done that consistently throughout my personal relationships, I might not be heading into retirement on my own. I have attended enough firefighters retirements, both On Call and Career firefighters, to know that the thought of retirement for most firefighters, either on medical grounds or reaching mandatory retirement age, comes with the realisation that part of one's identity will be lost. I will no longer be a firefighter, being prepared for anything to protect the irreplaceable. All fire services realise that each individual firefighter has considerable personal 'skin in the game'. The uniform, the organisation, the colleagues, they become part of who you are. At some stage for every firefighter there will be internal personal conflict between who they are as private citizens and their public commitment to being a firefighter. This conflict will be complicated by diminishing resources compelling organisations to continually change the way they do business to resource the service to the community. Sometimes efficiency comes at the price of effectiveness.

The key to managing the conflict is ensuring a balance between identities. There is a personal identity and a uniform identity. The latter shrouds the outer self which, over time, has become embedded in the inner self. Any imbalance will be resolved at point of employment separation of vocational retirement. Recognising this personal dilemma, Fire and Rescue NSW is presently introducing a program named 'Code 4'. It is an analogy: the fire or rescue emergency is over and the crew is returning to the station. The Code 4 program is being designed to assist firefighters in the transition associated with leaving the service, including separation from their identity as a firefighter. It is about providing information on maintaining health and wellbeing, preparing to embrace new interests, creating friendship networks and offering information forums to keep former members updated on happenings within the service. The program will grow and position firefighters for healthy and constructive exit from their former career.

Final thought

For successful leadership in such a dynamic occupation as firefighting, leaders need to consider the whole person—body, mind and spirit. They must also attend to the personal dimensions that flow from the identity that being a firefighter creates. Each challenge comes to an end. This is true regardless of the duration, magnitude or personal significance of the challenge. When one challenge is completed, it is time to move onto the next challenge, learning and moving forward.

References

S Curnin, B Brooks and C Owens, 'A case study of disaster decision-making in the presence of anomalies and absence of recognition', University of Tasmania, Hobart, 2020.

J Fewtrell, 'Foundational Qualities for Fire Service Crew Commanders', IFE Conference, 2010.

G Klein, 'A recognition-primed decision (RPD) model of rapid decision making', pp. 138–147, in J Gary Klein, R C Orasanu & C. Zsambok (eds), *Decision making in action: Models and methods*, Ablex Publishing, 1993.

2 Values and a people focus: Ambulance Victoria

Rebecca Hodges

*A*mbulance Victoria (AV) is Victoria's only state-wide health service. It looks after 6.5 million people in metropolitan, regional and rural Victoria, across 273,000 square kilometres in Australia's fastest growing state. AV responds to over 650,000 emergency cases every year, with a workforce greater than 6,500 supported by fleet both on the road and in the air. AV services to the Victorian community include emergency health care, stroke telemedicine, transfer of complex adult and paediatric patients, secondary triage and referral services, and non-emergency transport. With such a diverse service base, AV attracts people from all parts of the community to explore both clinical and non-clinical career pathways.

Workforce demographics have changed considerably over the last two decades. In 2008, Ambulance Victoria was formed through the amalgamation of two ambulance services, the Metropolitan Ambulance Service and Rural Ambulance Victoria. At the time the newly formed AV looked very different. It hosted a workforce of 4,229. Women comprised only 35 percent of the workforce while 73 percent of management positions were occupied by men. Fast forwarding to 2020, the workforce has grown to 7,120. Of new recruits, 89.5 percent are part of AV's graduate pathway starting their career as Advanced Life Support (ALS) paramedics. In 2019–2020, 61 percent of all graduate paramedics were women. Some 71 percent of the workforce is under the age of 44 years, accounting for 78 percent of the broader AV workforce.

Women comprise approximately 50 percent of the overall workforce and now hold 35 percent of leadership positions.

Workforce data indicates a disproportionate number of women working for AV from Generation Y (26 percent) as opposed to men, who, are more evenly spread across the Baby Boomer (11 percent), Generation X (16 percent) and Generation Z (20 percent) cohorts. There is an increasing number of employees, now 9 percent, representing the iGen generation. One in four men are aged over 55 years, with an additional one hundred and two men to turn 65 years old by the end of the next calendar year.

This provides data insight into AV's generational diversity profile and the composition of the workforce. This profile is the foundation of AV's people based functions and programs that are needed to support the workforce to morally and ethically engage with their work.

Qualitative recruitment data shows that the main driver in obtaining employment with AV is caring for patients and to work within the community. This has not changed over many years, nor has it been influenced by workforce generations or demographics.

Personal ambitions are somewhat difficult to gauge and understand as individuals want different things out of their careers at different times of their lives. AV has seen considerable transformation in its people systems that support activities such as transfer and promotion, flexible work arrangements and rostering. These functions were traditionally designed for a male workforce who were able to focus on career development and progression.

Coupled with a steady increase in female participation since the amalgamation, the attraction of more women into paramedicine has been driven by tertiary qualifications requirements. The increase of women in the AV workforce has meant that AV has needed to change and accept different workforce models and programs. It was, and still is, essential that AV leadership acknowledges the need to recognise the professional and personal needs of women.

Although there is gender balance in the overall workforce this is not reflected in leadership roles. Recent promotional processes saw women being promoted into senior operational positions. This was achieved through a centralised process in which unconscious bias principles were applied through the recruit smarter program lead by the Victorian Department of Premier and Cabinet. What was observed was that when promotional processes were free from all forms of bias the women performed at the same level as the men, if not better.

It is important to note that even though the performance of women in the promotional processes improved, there is little difference in the number of women being appointed into senior operational leadership positions. This is evidenced when comparing the data at the time of the amalgamation to current day. This suggests that there is still considerable work to be done to support women to progress through their career. This could be an aspect where women could feel that the organisation has not been supportive in the same way it has been for their male colleagues.

The recently negotiated Paramedic Enterprise Agreement is an example of how an industrial instrument can support and enhance individuals work life experiences and alignment of values. Considering that 61 percent of AV's graduate cohort are women, it is important to recognise that to enable women to fully participate in the workforce there is a need to provide for it through the industrial instrument. There are specific clauses that deal with pay equity, workplace flexibility and career progression.

The inter-generational profile is a point worthy of reflection. If you consider the growth in workforce numbers since 2008, with an attrition rate of less than 5 percent, it tells us that the vast majority of the workforce has one single employer for their entire professional career. There are layers of complexity when thinking about values and what attracts individuals to an organisation. Individuals effectively grow and mature not only as professionals but as people. The values held by an experienced workforce are different to that of a less experienced one. AV has five generations spanning its workforce, all with different values and morals relating to work. The IGen, Gen Z and X want a workplace that supports flexibility, accelerated career pathways, learning and technology. Whereas the baby boomers started in an organisation based on formal structures, seniority and different cultural norms. AV has responded to the difference in generations through target programs such as transition to retirement, all roles flex and the establishment of the Diversity and Inclusion council.

The professional alignment between individuals and the profession are supported by formal structures such as professional registration. In 2018 paramedics became a registered profession with the Australian Health Practitioner Regulation Agency.

The Paramedicine Board of Australia code of conduct clearly articulates the important standards for practitioner behaviour in terms of:

- Providing good care, including shared decision making;
- Working with patients or clients;
- Working with practitioners;
- Working within the healthcare system;
- Minimising risk;
- Maintaining professional performance;
- Professional behaviour and ethical conduct;
- Ensuing practitioner health;
- Teaching, supervision and assessing, and
- Research[1]

The Board's Code of conduct explains the intersection of personal and professional values and qualities. This provides a framework and connection for individuals joining AV and the paramedic profession. Further to the paramedic becoming a registered profession, the workforce of AV is part of the Victorian public sector. This provides another aspect of intersection between personal and professional values. AV is bound by the *Public Service Administration Act*; the act outlines a number of key requirements of all public entities but in particular the requirement to adhere to the core public sector values.

In 2017 AV was subject to an IBAC investigation—Operation Tone. The investigation focussed on allegations that paramedics engaged in serious corrupt conduct, namely the theft, trafficking and use of drugs of dependence, and misappropriation of AV equipment. The investigation identified a culture of illicit drug use and misappropriation of AV equipment by individuals and among certain groups in a specific location.[2]

This is concerning from a number of different perspectives, in particular in the context of AV's Patient Commitment and organisational values. The investigation found that:

illicit drug use, possession and trafficking are criminal offences and not in line with Code of Conduct for Victorian Public Sector Employees and the AV Workplace Conduct Policy;

the use of drugs of dependence undermines the safety of the Victorian community. It is imperative that a paramedic's judgement and performance not be impaired by illicit drugs; and

the use of drugs of dependence impacts public confidence in AV.

This investigation highlighted disconnection between our organisational based values and morals compared to localised conduct and values. The local workplace had created its own cultural norms and values that were in conflict with not only the values and Code of Conduct of AV but also those of the Victorian Public Sector.

The outcomes of this investigation were difficult to manage as in some cases the individuals involved did not understand the impact of their behaviours and actions. This is because of what was accepted as local norms or behaviours. This caused considerable disharmony and division within AV at the time. It was important that response was focused on leadership, accountability, learning and reflection. Tony Walker, Chief Executive Officer, led the discussion reminding the entire workforce of our commitment to our code of conduct and the connection with the public sector. In relation to specific individuals, where appropriate, the outcomes of the professional conduct processes supported participation in ethical and moral based development and coaching. This was to provide individuals with the opportunity to reconnect their values and morals and realign with the AV and Public Sector values and Codes of Conduct. Although this was a challenging experience it enabled growth and reflection. It tested values and moral alignment and between AV and its people. A targeted communication and education package was rolled out across AV to support the workforce in understanding individual responsibilities. This was underpinned by strong and transparent leadership, both locally and organisationally.

Like many Australian Health Services, AV has reinvented itself to meet the changing demands of the community and its workforce. The workforce demographic data shows the intergenerational challenges that AV experiences with its people support systems, programs and initiatives to meet the needs of all parts of the workforce and individuals. Overlaying values and morals, alignment both individually and organisationally creates a workforce conundrum.

To manage the complexity and address individual career developmental needs, AV has implemented person centred workforce strategies and frameworks. Supported by the employee life cycle, AV has recognised that each individual's needs are different and therefore require flexibility in response. There has been an intentional effort to mirror the patient care model (patient centred care) within the workforce. The alignment has provided the opportunity to build on a culture that not only focuses on patients but also on its people as well.

AV's approach to the Mental Health and Wellbeing of its workforce demonstrates the commitment to its people and the alignment of both the patient and workforce models of care and commitment. The AV Mental Health and Wellbeing Strategy focuses on the psychological risks associated with first response work. It provides different clinical and wellbeing services dependant on the needs of the individual.

In 2019, AV conducted the second online Psycho-social Survey, this enables a better understanding of the health and wellbeing needs of AV staff and volunteers, thereby informing future mental health initiatives. This survey was first conducted in 2016 and is planned to be re-issued biennially. Results from 1,333 respondents indicated that a small but significant proportion of the workforce experiences mental health concerns, such as mood symptoms, psychological distress, PTSD, alcohol use and suicidal thoughts. Generally, high levels of support-seeking, particularly informal supports, were found. However, respondents also indicated a number of barriers to seeking and utilising supports, suggesting organisational stigma remains an issue. Comparisons with the inaugural 2016 Psycho-social Health and Wellbeing Survey found increases in measures such as symptoms of depression, anxiety and stress, psychological distress and sleep difficulties. Similarly, a number of organisational and occupational stressors also increased over time, which may be reflective of operational restructures and changes within AV occurring during the collection period.

The survey has identified a few key areas of concern, and highlighted the need for quality interventions and treatments to be implemented in the *2019–2022 Mental Health Action Plan*. AV has recognised the importance of family as an integral support structure for its workforce, in particular recognising early signs of mental health injury such as Post Traumatic Stress Disorder (PTSD). AV has launched its own family engagement plan that provides an inclusive pathway for families to be involved in the care of their loved ones. AV Family Safe Space provides AV family members with helpful evidence-based resources and support needed to support family members (AV employee or volunteer) or dependents. The aim of this site is also to provide information about the stressors that can be faced on the job, whether for corporate or operational staff members.

AV participates yearly in the Victorian Public Sector People Matters Survey. Essentially this survey measures employee engagement and other aspects of the employee experience. It is an evidence based tool that provides insights into how the workforce is feeling and is a learning opportunity for AV. It facilitates the opportunity to evaluate the effectiveness and impact of workforce initiatives along with the basis for future program design. In 2019 there was a significant uplift in the completion rate to 50 percent, up from 27 percent in 2018. The engagement index has improved over the last four years, achieving a score of 70 in 2019 compared to a score of 48 in 2014. The 2019 survey results show that there is a deep connection to professional pride and a strong element to performance and delivery. This is a critical observation that is linked to the implementation of strategic patient initiatives.

The AV strategic plan provides insight into how the corporate narrative is linked to an operating environment that is constantly changing and increasingly complex. The vision of the strategic plan 'Outstanding emergency health care every time' is supported by the AV Patient Care Commitment:

We save lives and improve lives by providing outstanding care for our patients. Our Patient Care Commitment is our promise to every patient and sits at the heart of everything we do.

The plan seeks four strategic outcomes: first, an exceptional patient experience; second, partnerships that make a difference; third, a great place to work and volunteer, and; fourth, high performing organisations. These outcomes are pursued through an implementation plan which encompasses program management and governance arrangements and details specific actions and responsibilities that connect specific programs of work.

The 2019 VPSC People Matters survey indicated that around 90 percent of respondents thought that:

- being responsive, working as a team and delivering quality services are all sources of pride for our people
- there is a strong element of performance and delivery which is critical to the organisational outcomes and delivering best care
- that there is strong team spirit at AV, and pride that people work together to for the best outcomes

It is clear from the results of the People Matters survey that implementing the AV strategic plan has helped to embed the corporate narrative in workplace culture. It has connected the corporate strategy and everyday life for our staff. People understand the connection and importance of their work in fulfilling AV's charter. It has shifted patient safety to the forefront of AV's values and the way it operates. This shift is directly correlated with why people choose to become paramedics, and the shared values and professional codes that undergird paramedic service. It is also important to acknowledge that connecting patients and frontline services shapes the mindset of AV's non-operational support departments. Every staff member is aware that their work is important because it contributes either directly or indirectly to patient care. Foregrounding this principle is a feature of AV's evolving culture and values.

Alongside our patients are our people. A key component of the strategic plan concerns staff health, safety and wellbeing which also influence patient care and service delivery. Over the previous few years, the workplace safety culture within AV normalised certain behaviours and accepted the incidence of injury. During 2014 nearly half of the operational workforce reported some form of workplace injury. Although this was a time of industrial unrest, when reporting higher levels of injury might have been related to collective bargaining for better pay and conditions, the workforce believed and management conceded that getting injured was just part of the job.

In 2016, AV launched its first health and safety strategy. It focused on building a better safety culture and addressing the three biggest safety risks: manual handling, psychological injury and occupational violence. Consistent with the mental health and wellbeing strategy, the health and safety culture was person-centred and developed in consultation with the workforce. The most significance element in these strategies was articulating to the workforce that the organisation, particularly the executive and senior leadership, were concerned for their wellbeing—body, mind and spirit. It was an opportunity to build trust across the workforce. The senior and executive leadership was proactive in promoting a safety first culture not only for patients but for the workforce as well.

The decisive factor was the personal and professional endorsement of the Chief Executive Office, Tony Walker. He spoke openly and candidly about the importance he placed on the safety and wellbeing of his colleagues. His firm leadership, based on a practical appreciation of the many workplace challenges, resonated deeply with the workforce. It gave AV a capacity for candid and sometimes controversial conversations that propelled a transformation of attitudes towards safety and led to changes in whole systems. This capacity provided the catalyst for the launch of AV's response to occupational violence. The centrepiece was a program that included innovative training, clinical practice changes, legislative change and a public messaging program that prompted a sector wide campaign to prevent violence against health care workers. Tony Walker's message was uncomplicated: 'we will not tolerate any violence towards you, and your safety is our highest priority'.

The 2019 survey results revealed strong endorsement of leadership behaviours. Put simply, leaders and managers are making key issues a priority and influencing the perceptions of employees, particularly in areas of workplace safety, respect, diversity, sharing of information, strategic alignment and role clarity. Workplace ethics are a set of values and moral principles pursued by both employers and employees. Workplace morals are essentially cultural standards that define how things should work. For the greatest part they are supported by personal experience and individual behaviours.

Like all public institutions, AV upholds and promotes public sector values and the codes of conduct that give these values a practical expression. And like most large organisations, these values and codes influence the way people behave and influence their interactions with other members of the workforce. The goal of the Victorian Public Sector Commission is for 'employees to understand the values and principles; managers to apply and encourage the applications; and, senior leaders to demonstrate and reinforce them as part of the culture of their organisation'. AV has built a deep connection with its workforce and created a strong of sense of community and of belonging.

The workforce has conscientiously embraced the 'Patient Care Commitment' which is expressed in organisational systems of work, strategic programs and initiatives, leadership development and governance arrangements. The consistent theme in AV's workplace values and moral principles is that everybody in the organisation has a contribution to make.

Moral and ethical connection with patient safety is foundational. In terms of the employee life cycle, for the university graduate patient safety is a value. It embodies a personal need to care for the community. For a qualified paramedic, personal and professional values start to intersect and then align. The primary function of an AV leader is connecting strategy, values and care. This connection, and it is an intimate one, creates a sense of belonging and imparts a vision of community. The alignment of values, behaviours and strategy ensures that the workforce shares common goals, standards and convictions. Unsurprisingly, difficulty arises when individuals ignore, overlook or act contrary to AV's values, codes and standards. Such behaviour not only leads to inner conflict, but also will work against any sense of team spirit and will harm AV's reputation within the community. Those who are the recipients of care will then wonder whether AV is reliable and trustworthy.

The following case study explores the impact of individual behaviour on organisational values and morals. AV terminated a paramedic for serious and wilful misconduct following the findings of an investigation by an external investigator into the attendance of the paramedic to a teenage boy presenting with cardiac arrest. The boy had tried to hang himself. The allegations concerned the senior paramedic's failure, as the most senior paramedic and scene leader, to take all reasonable steps in caring for the health and safety of the patient. The senior paramedic directed the treating paramedics to cease their resuscitation efforts prior to the minimum expected timeframe of 30 minutes. She was aware that it was premature to cease resuscitation and knew there were compelling reasons to continue, such as the patient's age and signs of life. The senior paramedic unreasonably dismissed the advice regarding the 'compelling reasons to continue resuscitation provided by an attending paramedic shortly after the arrival at scene'. The senior paramedic misled the patient's family about the benefits of continuing to resuscitate the patient shortly after she arrived on the scene.

At the time of dismissal, the senior paramedic had been employed by AV for nearly 19 years. She lodged an unfair dismissal claim with the Fair Work

Commission for reinstatement and loss of wages. The Commission's Deputy President determined that the dismissal was not hard, unjust or unreasonable as the application was dismissed. The senior paramedic claimed she had adequately discharged her duties and AV was not able reflect on her performance or behaviour.

This case study reveals that AV's Patient Commitment was not at the centre of how this senior paramedic provided on-scene support or care for this patient. The senior paramedic was in charge at the scene and influenced inexperienced paramedics through her presence and seniority. But why did the senior paramedic not conduct herself to operate in a manner that reflected AV's organisational outlook? The answer points to the alignment of personal and professional morals and values. The senior paramedic appeared to have little insight at that moment of what constituted professional conduct or acceptable patient treatment. AV's response demonstrates the depth of organisational commitment to its values and, in particular, its commitment to patients and the Victorian community. This incident certainly challenged the workforce. It unsettled parts of the workforce who struggled to understand how one of their own, a professional dedicated to saving the lives of others, stopped resuscitating a patient who was showing signs of life. It was incomprehensible. AV's most senior and experienced paramedics were critical of their former colleagues conduct, reiterating the shared commitment to patient safety and exceptional clinical care.

Finally, AV's values and morals are grounded in its commitment to its patients and the workforce. Achieving excellence is not enough. It needs to be maintained. AV has embraced the challenge of continuous change even when organisational transformation is uncomfortable or confronting. But the importance of aligning values, morals and strategy in the form of service delivery is made plain in what the organisation has learned from internal surveys. Critical, too, is firm and conscientious leadership, particularly from the Chief Executive Officer and senior operational executives. This kind of leadership has enabled AV to learn and evolve. Industrial unrest and a depleted workforce are things of the past, which is now a distant place. There are occasional echoes of the way things were done but they now fail to resonate. Both the leadership and the workforce have embraced a culture in which shared values and common aspirations have ensured a tight focus on a commitment to care for people—whether patients or colleagues.

Endnotes

1   Accessed 26 June 2020 <http://ahpra.gov.au>.

2   Accessed 28 June 2020. <http:/ibac.vic.gov.au>.

References

Independent broad-based anti-Corruption Commission, viewed 28 June 2020. https://www.ibac.vic.gov.au/publications-and-resources/HTML/ operation-tone-special-report.

Ambulance Victoria Strategic Plan, 2017–2022, Outstanding emergency health care every time.

Ambulance Victoria People Matters Survey Results 2019.

The Australian Health Practitioner Regulation Agency (AHPRA), viewed 3 June 2020, Paramedicine Board of Australia, Code of conduct 2018. https://www.paramedicineboard.gov.au/Professional-standards/Codes-guidelines-and-policies/Code-of-conduct.aspx.

Ambulance Victoria Mental Action Plan 2019–2022.

3   Ethical heroism and emergency services leadership

Mark Crosweller

*O*ver the past 36 years I have had the great privilege of working with many inspiring people in local communities, the private sector, and the public sector at the local, state, national and international level. My career started in 1981, initially in design, construction and engineering in the private sector. In January 1985 I joined what was then known as the New South Wales Bushfire Brigades as an unpaid volunteer, remaining a volunteer while rising through the ranks from Basic Firefighter to Deputy Group Captain. I was recruited into the salaried ranks of the fire service as an Inspector in 1994 followed by a promotion to District Superintendent in 1996.

I was again promoted, this time to Assistant Commissioner, at the end of 1998, leading various portfolios until late 2009 when appointed Commissioner for the Australian Capital Territory Emergency Services Agency. In December 2012 I became Director General of Emergency Management Australia. This was an Australian Government post. I fulfilled this role until April 2018 when appointed as Head of the National Resilience Taskforce, another Australian Government post.

After being promoted to Inspector in 1994, I commenced a long career in crisis, national security and emergency management. For over 20 years I was an executive leader working with or for senior and chief executives, local councillors and mayors, state and federal ministers, as well as prime ministers and their respective governments, on matters relating to strategy, policy, operations, risk and resilience within complex, ambiguous and uncertain environments.

Throughout that journey, I witnessed and experienced some of humanity's deepest sorrows and greatest joys as events played out across our country and elsewhere in the world that were prompted by merciless nature or human failing. I saw some of the best human beings had to offer, and I saw some of the worst. Irrespective of their position or role within organisations, I realised that most people were trying to do the best they could within the boundaries of both their internal and external limitations, often in the most dire circumstances. This has been my approach, too.

What follows is an insight into my experiences and my appreciation of the critical role that ethics have played in the leadership I have endeavoured to exert. I will present a personal perspective on why there has been a steady decline in the importance of virtue ethics within the practice of leadership over that same period. Finally, I will offer some suggestions for reclaiming these virtues for the exercise of our own leadership and for the benefit of those we serve. I have tried to be candid while trying to avoid referring to any specific organisation or particular individual in any manner that might identify them.

Setting the scene

Throughout most of my career, the organisations that I have worked within were generally established either directly or indirectly by the Australian Constitution and the subsequent laws, policies and strategies of respective governments at local, state, and national level. Unlike the private sector where my career began, public institutions do not need to 'work out where they fit'. They do not need to do market appraisals, develop competitive products and services, or compete for market share and profitability for their survival. Their role and remit is handed to them by government. At least at the macro level, their 'reason for being' is well established in a legal and administrative sense and usually embedded into the fabric of modern Australian society. Their vision, mission and purpose is achieving the greatest good (expressed in practical outcomes) for the greatest number of people (described as the public) in a manner that is defined by the democratically-elected government. Theoretically at least, these organisations have a clear mandate. They were established by the will of the people to promote the public interest and pursue the common good. The service element is often what draws people to these organisations. Their mission aligns closely with a person's sense of meaning, purpose, and identity.

They also conduct their activities according to 'rules'. These rules often encompass laws, regulations, principles, policies, procedures and processes that give shape to administrative structures and formal responsibilities. These mechanisms are often referred to as the 'machinery of government'. There is more than an irony in this description. Some scholars argue they are in every sense a 'machine'. The former head of the London School of Economics, Anthony Giddens, refers to them as 'juggernauts; massive inexorable forces, objects, or movements that either sweep up or crush whatever is in their path. Their influence is extensive, their direction unstoppable'. My experience over 35 years leads me to concur with this metaphor, as I will explain.

Operating within the context of 'rules' and 'outcomes' in normative ethical theory usually means to operate through the ethics of deontology (rules) and utilitarianism/consequentialism (outcomes). There is, however, a third element and it is arguably more important in leadership. I am referring here to virtue ethics (character). All three normative ethical theories are important and necessary for effective institutions and functioning societies. But while deontological and utilitarian/consequentialist approaches rely principally on rational thought to determine behaviour, virtue ethics relies upon the development and education over time of the virtues through reason, perception, emotion, and action. These attributes assist in building relationships between people and contribute to organisational culture.

Enter the 'machine'

The emergency services sector travelled a very difficult road between the mid-1990s and 2013. During that period, leaders had progressively separated themselves from their communities in subtle but important ways. The sector had transitioned from 'protecting citizens and keeping them safe' to 'it is a dangerous world and you (the citizen) need to be resilient'. This was triggered by an ideological shift across the broader political landscape that is often attributed to Margaret Thatcher and her famous insistence that

> there is no such thing as society. There are individual men and women, and there are families. And no government can do anything except

through people, and people must look to themselves first. It's our duty to look after ourselves and then, also to look after our neighbour. People have got the entitlements too much in mind, without the obligations. There's no such thing as entitlement, unless someone has first met an obligation.

Politics across modern western democracies such as Australia, the United Kingdom and the United States transitioned their economies and societies to the desire for smaller government, contestability, deregulation, and out-sourcing. This desire, coupled with aggressive market intervention, pursued economic efficiency, effectiveness, and productivity across all aspects of society. The greatest good for the greatest number was prioritised towards economic gains. Sharing in these gains called for citizens to be more individualist, entrepreneurial, and self-sufficient to relieve the burdens they otherwise placed upon governments, their institutions and ultimately other taxpayers.

More specifically, individuals were to be increasingly responsible for their personal safety by being resilient to an array of hazards, threats and perils. Their reward was reduced taxation, regulatory intervention and increased control over their lives by governments. Instead, citizens were afforded, through active participation in the marketplace, the necessary social and economic circumstances to exercise their agency for self-protection and self-sustainment. That is, the ability to exercise free will and personal choice in determining what was good and right for them in any given circumstance, albeit in the context of an increasingly dangerous world. All of this reinforced material individualism where self-interest, economic independence and economic success were seen (and still are) as the highest personal aspirations. Survival of the fittest was to be the order of the day. A failure to protect oneself in adversity, or to sustain oneself more generally both economically and socially, was viewed as being morally irresponsible.

So powerful and pervasive was this shift that the 'machinery of government' was fundamentally altered in response to support these objectives. Regrettably, emergency services Leaders and their organisational cultures, often at the direction of their governments, embraced this approach with enthusiasm. Unconsciously, they effectively placed a wedge between themselves and the citizens they were charged with protecting. Instead, leaders were expected to comply with this agenda and deliver its political imperatives.

Learning some bitter lessons

The effect of such distancing was to play out numerous times during a series of major crises. In the days leading up to the catastrophic Canberra bushfires of January 2003, emergency services leaders assured the community, over-confidently in my view, that they could contain the fire. Citizens were told they need not worry, providing that they had adequately prepared themselves and their properties. This kind of posturing reflected the attitude of many within the emergency services sector at the time although there were a few discordant voices. They struggled to be heard and were largely ignored. The devastation suffered by the national capital revealed overconfident attitudes and mistaken assumptions. The result was the deaths of four people and the destruction of 488 homes in one afternoon. Public trust and community confidence in the ACT's emergency services were damaged for much longer.

Fast forward to February 2009 and Victoria. The state faced some of its worst fire weather in recorded history. Again, among many contributing factors that led to failure in the eyes of many citizens, was the presumption that everyone had, or should have had, an adequate fire plan to protect themselves. Of course, many did not for a host of reasons including economic and social disadvantage along with mental and physical health challenges. Tragically, these were either not known or were inadequately understood by many leaders. On 7 February 2009, 173 people perished and over 2000 homes were destroyed. This carnage occurred on a single afternoon. Once again, public trust and community confidence in government generally and in emergency services specifically were seriously depleted. On the eve of the ten-year anniversary in 2019, deep hurt and widespread suspicion remained within the worst affected communities.

A third example demonstrates the inability of public authorities to learn lessons from tragedies. On the afternoon of 6 February 2011, the Roleystone-Kelmscott fire in Western Australia destroyed 86 homes. Thankfully, no lives were lost. Although there was an expectation that citizens were well prepared, the management of this fire was considered so poor that the government commissioned a special inquiry, removed both the Chief Executive and Chief Officer from their positions, decommissioned the extant Fire and Emergency Services Authority, re-wrote the relevant legislation and established a new government department. Here was another significant breach of public trust and community confidence that could not be explained away. Major reforms were required.

While various commissions of inquiry concluded the causes of these breaches of trust and confidence were many and varied, one consistent factor was the wedge that had been driven between the leader and the citizen. This wedge distanced the leader from the citizen and contributed to tipping the scales away from the more discerning ethical aspects of virtue towards a subtle, perhaps even unconscious bias, towards overconfidence and detachment that took the form of pursuing an agenda focused on citizen responsibility and individual resilience.

In profound ways, leaders had inadvertently lost sight of what it really meant to be trusted, what it meant for others to suffer, and what they could do about it. The ideological and systemic shift from 'keeping people safe' to 'it is a dangerous world and you need to be prepared', separated the leaders from the led. The importance of a close relationship with the citizenry was overlooked or undervalued. The loss of this close relationship was to have a devastating effect on many leaders who had sincerely believed they were doing the right things for the right reasons. Having been criticised for a breach of their own moral and ethical duty in the service of others, it was incredibly painful to witness their professional demise and personal distress.

From the moral to the amoral

Most ideologies are little more than strategies. There is no-one 'pulling the strings' to promote a comprehensive or consistent agenda. Ideologies are both consciously and unconsciously driven by many factors and forces, including political and institutional leaders, with the main message morphing all too easily over time into purported 'common sense'. The social and cultural influences flowing from them are taken for granted and eventually normalised. Most of us fall into the trap of believing ideological principles are self-evident, manifestations of nature that are rational and worthwhile, especially when there is an element of self-interest or the existing order delivers power and privilege.

Throughout my senior executive career I have watched leaders becoming increasingly enslaved to absorbing the annual minimum 2 percent efficiency dividend while simultaneously attempting to increase productivity, reduce waste, negate political exposure, mitigate risk and increase the resilience of citizens. These goals seemed sensible in the first year. But 20 years on, and continuing to seek similar efficiencies and productivity increases, not to mention explaining that the world was becoming even more dangerous, it seems like entrenched institutional madness.

The progressive draining of program funding and discretionary spending was relentless in too many organisations. Disinterest in effectiveness masked obsession with efficiency. The scramble for funding pitched leader against leader, agency against agency, state against state, and every state against the Commonwealth. This scramble would turn otherwise collaborative environments into competitive battlefields. Organisations became toxic as political, operational, and administrative leaders elevated debates over funding and the allocation of financial liability to the apex of corporate concerns. Any consideration of good public policy developed in the interests of enhancing the well-being of the citizenry was usually overlooked. Many public-spirited leaders would leave high-level meetings feeling bitter, angry and frustrated as their commitment to creative and imaginative public interest policies were thwarted by agency greed, jurisdictional self-interest and the resulting stalemate over money.

Organisational narratives were not immune from this agenda. Efficiency and effectiveness, protecting 'the system', and not wanting citizens to be reliant upon government for support by encouraging self-resilience in every circumstance, were dominant influences. These narratives were conflated with stories of a 'more dangerous world' which were being driven partly by a changing climate or by climate change, depending upon the prevailing political opinion. That natural disaster seasons were becoming longer, more intense and more frequent was noted for additional effect.

Political risk aversion was also prominent. 'The minister wants no surprises' was often chanted, implying that most strategies were not to be pursued unless there was a guarantee that there would be no political fallout. This was understandable, especially if you were a minister. I agreed with the need for prudence on one level. I struggled, however, when departmental officials took this principle to the extreme and confidently spoke on behalf of the minister when I knew full well they had no idea what the minister might have thought nor understood what risks the minister might have been prepared to accept. In fact, most had never met their minister! I also witnessed leaders increasingly compromising their sense of duty to the citizenry and their own workforce (volunteer or paid) to prioritise the economy, the budget, institutional sovereignty and political populism. Many were uncomfortable with this kind of compromise even as they complied with a range of extraneous pressures and secondary demands.

At the same time, career progression for senior executives moved away from deep subject matter expertise balanced with, for example, exemplary human resource and strategic management competencies. Instead, career success was measured more by a move towards what I would call an *amoral* stance of political compliance to the wishes of the government of the day. Many argued that frank and fearless politically contextualised advice had become increasingly unwelcome while fulfilling the expectations of populist politics seemed to be more pressing. Let me stress that an amoral stance does not mean an immoral one. Notably, the word 'amoral' denotes an indifference to moral considerations whereas, in this context, the word 'immoral' implies a conscious decision to say or do something that is believed to be wrong or motivated by evil intent. I am not suggesting that leaders were intentionally doing the wrong thing or conniving to do bad things. I am contending, however, that a growing and predominant amoral influence meant that consideration of values and virtues was relegated to the private realm of individuals. This influence spawned a culture that effectively precluded them from exercising public leadership or offering contrary views on where the common good might reside. As organisational leaders they had been subordinated to a set of rules and an inventory of outcomes that placed economic gains, career progression and political populism at the forefront of their thinking and acting.

Out with the virtues, in with the injury
Consequently, upholding whatever was good, right, and just within the life of their organisation, supported by character virtues such as humility and compassion, was steadily devalued and diminished in profile. This drift left organisational cultures exposed to the effects of an amoral individualism that was perpetrated by both leaders and followers. Additionally, moral integrity, personal meaning and vocational purpose had been narrowed in favour of pursuing status and progress within a careerist framework. This rearrangement of what was collectively esteemed caused many individuals and, indeed, whole institutions, to lose sight of the constitutional mandate and legal obligation to serve and protect the citizenry as a first-order duty.

Further, these same individuals and institutions neglected or overlooked the need for virtue ethics in delivering a vitally important public service.

In my view, the process of re-prioritising, de-valuing and narrowing the collective commitment to virtue ethics was among the main causes of 'moral injury'. The dominant ideological agendas and the associated narratives that legitimised them, also served to undermine the altruism that propels most people to join police, emergency services and national security agencies. The majority join to serve the public interest and to protect the common good but are often obliged to comply with policies and procedures that seem anti-thetical to the corporate goals being pursued and contrary to their reason for joining. Ultimately, they serve and protect the self-perpetuating 'machine' that many organisations become when they lose sight of the public and a service ethos. Most people within the organisation are able to rationalise this compromise and accommodate their disappointment with varying degrees of personal and professional discomfort. For others, however, what they observe or experience of organisational life offends their ethical sensibilities and unsettles their moral compass. Such discomfort, when pushed to the limits of human toleration, has a substantial bearing on individual well-being and organisational health.

Righteous heroism

Neither leaders nor followers are immune from the effects of amoral individualism. Reinforcing a distorted righteousness is one of them. Despite the pervasive effects of ideology, many services, agencies and departments manage to avoid descending into ethical chaos and moral darkness. They want to do good things and they continue to serve the public and its interests. But the committed righteous leader or follower might not acknowledge the reality that organisations are capable of doing good and being bad. Police, emergency services and national security culture can be blighted by an overly simplistic differentiation of right and wrong, predicated on self-interest and private opinion. 'I/we am/are on the side of good, you/they are not' is one way of illustrating this mindset. 'White knight on noble steed' is another. Although this is neither the expressed nor implied view of the leader and their senior executive team, it is not rigorously challenged. This mistaken mindset is left and allowed to persist in the realm of silence. The void created by the absence of a clear ethical narrative and a firm moral example from the leadership can be filled by these distorted views.

Throughout my career I have noticed that some individuals become right-eously heroic when their mistaken view of the organisation is not challenged. They steadily become too literal and unbending in their perspectives of what constitutes 'good versus evil'. Almost inevitably, they become strongly opinionated on 'how things ought to be' and 'what the world should be like', but are rather uninterested in the deeper aspects of 'why' the world (and its people) are that way. The 'why' question is, of course, much harder to answer because it implies having to develop the capacity to think reflectively and self-critically. It also requires a well-developed sense of compassion coupled with a good measure of wisdom in being able to appreciate the plight of others. Additionally, having to decide what could reasonably or, perhaps, even unrea-sonably, be done about the plight of others is the foremost demand imposed on a leader. A commitment to virtue is pursued alongside observance of the rules and attentiveness to the outcome.

In such circumstances, righteous heroes, instead of being reflective and flexible, are sometimes disruptive and rigid. They generally refuse to yield to alternative views, convinced their position is right and just, even masterful. From their perspective, the organisation is simply wrong. There is no appeas-ing them. Their demands are unreasonable, usually more about power and privilege than moral reasoning and ethical principles. Often, their narratives are not challenged by executives who might be insufficiently familiar with ethically complex situations, unsure of their own ethical foundations and how to defend them, lacking the confidence to take a firm stand on prin-ciple and fearful of the political fallout for doing something that might be unpopular. Appeasing all of the competing parties is often the outcome. And yet appeasement only serves to entrench disruption and rigidity. The toxicity of such a situation is not addressed and the organisational culture remains poisonous. Further, those who were committed to navigating the ethical and moral tensions between themselves and their organisation are isolated and alienated. Generally, these situations quickly lead to absenteeism and then compensation claims and substantial payouts. In other words, they rarely end well or without significant organisational pain. Perhaps more concerning is the standing of people who are endeavouring to alleviate personal 'ethical and moral discomfort' while the organisation's defects and deficiencies are completely overlooked.

Cultural heroism

I have also witnessed leaders and followers who have developed a deep moral and ethical conscience within organisations that, while still delivering on their stated public mandate and fulfilling basic expectations, had fallen for what I call 'cultural heroism'. I have in mind organisational cultures that overstate their worldly importance. These organisations have developed an excessive desire for recognition and reward. Their reputations and how they are seen by the community has an elevated status. In many ways this tendency is much more difficult to overcome because the tide of amoral individualism is too great a countervailing force. Rather than managing a few righteous individuals with distorted views of their ethics and morality, I have seen major contours in organisational culture move in this direction. These organisational cultures are, as might be expected, highly sensitive to criticism. They do not welcome critique, even in the form of constructive commentary.

At the same time, the organisation's leadership is still beholden to a sense of duty built on complying with an ideological agenda that is focussed on economic gains, career progression and political populism as the foremost corporate objectives. With these priorities in mind, if the 'rules' are followed and the 'outcomes' are delivered, standards of character are of relatively little importance. While these organisations are fulfilling their mandates in a formal sense, the cost is excessive when inclusive of sick leave, workers compensation and staff recruitment. But the hidden costs, the emotional and spiritual impacts, are much higher and leave a lasting deficit.

Bullying and intimidation are too often experienced by those who have a deep moral and ethical conscience but fear speaking out given a lack of personal courage at the senior executive level and the absence of a strong and consistent corporate narrative to support them. Instead, unethical behaviour can flourish in the shadows of culture. It is never far from view but never allowed into the light. Sadly, leaders who are, on some level, complicit with such behaviour are often promoted within these cultures. Perversely, policies, systems, processes and procedures tend to protect rather than challenge them. They are rarely, if ever, held to account. Doing so might damage the organisation's reputation and public confidence although its effectiveness and efficiency is gradually declining. If the organisation attempts to hold an individual to account for their behaviour, the tables are often turned against the organisation in favour of the individual. Attempting to remove a leader is often expensive. Hefty compensation payouts or full return to status are frequently the consequence of flawed processes that fail to hold leaders to account. A single procedural glitch or administrative lapse in the removal process is sufficient to reinforce a distorted sense of righteousness in the individual although he or she might lack moral integrity and have failed to uphold prescribed ethical standards. Conversely, this individual may be portrayed as a hero who stood against an executive leadership that was no friend of the workforce. In these situations, senior executive leaders are sadly without an effective response. They relied too much on the 'rules' to manage these situations and these rules were found to be wanting—bureaucratically and ethically.

Ethical heroism

What I have observed is not, however, all bad. I have also observed acts of heroism motivated by virtue. A key distinction between righteous heroism in contrast to ethical heroism is the absence of self-interest, self-importance and self-regard. Another is the leader's refined understanding of the virtues and how they can be utilised to achieve good outcomes within complex, uncertain and ambiguous environments. I have known leaders who have exhibited genuine and committed interest in the well-being of others and pursued positive actions to aid their followers in worthy pursuits. They have also acted to alleviate their sufferings. Sometimes this action was spontaneous and without conscious thought. At other times, this altruism was more subtle than overt, concealed in motivations and conveyed in disguise. Adversity has been recognised in all its forms, not just in the traditional sense of material loss or physical disability. Sometimes, leaders have risked their lives, not only literally, but also metaphorically. Their physical life was not threatened, but their professional future was on the line as the faced the prospect of their career dying.

Nevertheless, armed with virtue they acted with both wisdom and courage. While the stakes were high, so was their ability to understand how far they could go before falling to the temptations of pride and ego. They were politically astute, practically seasoned and understood legal and ethical thresholds while maximising the opportunities to do good for the well-being of others and for their organisations. When this occurred, the organisational culture responded in much the same way. Altruism promoted altruistic acts. Those who transcended themselves found their staff would follow them wherever they went, including to another organisation. Their energy was infectious, and people felt a genuine sense of purpose and meaning in their presence and under their stewardship.

Their narratives were inspiring because they were infused with consideration for others and a strong determination to do the right thing for the right reasons with wisdom derived from lived experience. This enabled them to impose an ethical narrative on a broad range of environmental complexities informing the context in which their organisations operated. They embodied their own ethical standards. It was not so much about what they said, although impressive, their actions were entirely consistent with their ethos. Operational and administrative leaders were generally admired by their superiors and political bosses, and the politicians by their constituencies.

The missing link

There are of course many reasons why individuals and organisations fail to fulfil ethical and moral expectations. Over the past 35 years I have observed the decline of organisational leadership. Rather than seeking to inform and influence their colleagues, many leaders have devoted more time and energy to subtly silencing and subordinating the voices of those emphasising the complex ethics of virtue that remain fundamental to character, culture and performance—institutionally and individually.

Trusting and being trusted, knowing, and expressing what we care about, who we care for, how we provide care, and how we receive it, are fundamental in determining how we treat others. Having compassion in seeing, understanding, and appreciating the suffering of other sentient beings while being prepared to reasonably, or perhaps even unreasonably, do something about that suffering must be the essence of keeping people safe and protecting their interests. Being grounded in thought, word, and action through an open mind that understands fallibility and imperfection while seeking to improve one's own performance, leads to better decision-making. Investing time, effort, and patience in understanding the true meaning of wisdom underpins all these ethics alongside addressing commonly-held fears of exploitation. Aligning thoughts, words, and actions towards the greater good of self and the other reinforces leadership integrity.

What a leader thinks, says and does shapes organisational culture and provides an example for others to embrace and follow. Followers are sometimes lacking in discrimination: they follow example whether it is good or bad. Ethical and moral attitudes and behaviours make a substantial contribution to a leader's identity, establishing a basis for the relationship with those they lead as well as informing the narratives that shape an evolving organisational culture. It is not until leaders return virtue ethics to its rightful and necessary place alongside deontological (rules) and utilitarian (outcome) ethics can we expect to see significant changes in organisational cultures. It is critical that organisations commit to continuing dialogue, education and training to ensure virtue ethics become integrated into the fabric of their organisational culture in contextualised and practical ways.

Fortunately, there are some vivid examples of this style of leadership, demonstrating what is possible. The leadership exercised by Nelson Mandela and Mahatma Ghandi show how virtue ethics played a critical role in the navigation of political and social complexity. More recently, the Prime Minister of New Zealand, Jacinda Ardern, has led her nation through a range of complex crises and social challenges through publicly stated and lived ethics of kindness, well-being and empathy. Although their execution has been imperfect, Ardern remains committed to their refinement and improvement while accepting the fallibility of her government. German Chancellor Angela Merkel and First Minister of Scotland Nicola Sturgeon are other good examples, placing the well-being of their citizens as the foremost objective and restructuring the 'rules', including their economies, to further the national need.

Conclusion

What makes virtue ethics so impressive when practised well is their significant contribution to inspiring, supporting, sustaining and motivating people to find meaning and purpose in their careers in support of institutional objectives and mandates. They also afford the opportunity to extend meaning and purpose into other aspects of life as well as countering the ill-winds that inevitably arise as part of the human journey. What is equally impressive but increasingly rare, is the level of courage and wisdom required to integrate virtue ethics into leadership and culture.

When left uncontested, the regrettably and pervasive effects of amoral individualism, economic prioritisation and political populism continue to erode the power and presence of virtue. This leads many to question their role within those organisations that are not active in countering this erosion, even as it undermines their original virtuous motivation which was to serve and protect the citizenry. Without a re-assertion of virtue ethics we should expect to see the persistence of cultures that feed dissatisfaction and despondency.

The task of contesting effects is not an invitation to advocate contesting causes. The ideologies arising from social and cultural influences that shape the mandates and priorities of our democracies and the institutions that deliver them, are beyond the contestation of individuals and organisational cultures. Leaders and followers remain responsible for navigating the complex tensions between personal ethical and moral priorities and those of their institutions. In this context, virtue ethics can alleviate some of these tensions by upholding and maintaining a close alignment between original motivations for joining an organisation and the corporate cultures that continue to support and nurture them. It can also ensure that a complete and transparent picture of the complex operating environment is articulated upon entry and sustained throughout the employment of a leader or follower. It can assist in achieving this outcome because it places the ethical and moral obligation for integrity, honesty and transparency upon the 'character' of the leadership, rather than just on the institutional 'rules' and 'outcomes'.

PART TWO

4　Silence and stigma: a law enforcement experience

Stephen Hayward

I can remember the Granville Train Disaster in 1977 like it was yester-day. I was 12 years old, and I was glued to the television screen. I was simply in awe at how the New South Wales Police Rescue Team placed themselves in harm's way to assist ordinary people, who hours beforehand, were simply on their daily commute to work. There was an immediate sense of knowing exactly what I wanted to be when I grew up. I had a sense of pride in their actions, and a hope that one day, 'I could be just like them'. If only I knew then what my life experiences and journey would bring, and who knows, perhaps, and more likely, it was very similar to at least one of those officers at that train site.

On 6 June 1986 I was on the parade ground at the Queensland Police Academy. Standing at attention in all my newly acquired uniform glory, I took the Oath of Service with my family looking on. In the weeks prior, the then-Police Commissioner, Sir Terence Lewis, and his wife had met us and provided an insight into the reality of policing life. I vividly remember Lady Lewis speaking to the wives and girlfriends on what to expect when their loved ones came home from work after seeing any number of ghastly crime scenes or accidents. Sir Terence spoke about the pride we should have in the uniform, the badge and how there was nothing more rewarding than dedicating yourself to duty to ensure society continued to function.

You also have another duty, and that is to each other. You will not be liked, and you must stick together. You owe it to each other, and to each other's families, to ensure that every day, you do your best to ensure that each and every one of you get to go home to their loved ones. You owe it to them. 'We were the fabric of society', he explained with conviction.

The Fitzgerald Commission of Inquiry had a devastating effect. That same once exalted individual was subsequently convicted, imprisoned on corruption charges and stripped of his knighthood. I was in the job only two years by then. I had served for six months in Townsville in Far North Queensland before I was transferred back to Brisbane. Stationed at the City Police Station, I was asked to do some 'undercover work' with the Licensing Branch. It involved visiting brothels and Starting Price (SP) 'bookie' dens. This was the first time where that shiny badge, the same one that, at the end of my career 16 years later, seemed to be such an integral part of my own identity, suddenly did not seem to have such a glow about it. I had joined the police to serve the people of Queensland although I was from New South Wales. Yet, I was a member of an organisation that had let those people down, and let them down badly. It was also the first time where I realised that one of my strongest core personal beliefs was one of integrity, which consists of doing the right thing when no one is looking. I was able to rationalise this conflict through my duties of uncovering the depths of prostitution and illegal gambling. I can still feel the dirty carpets of some of the establishments I visited where there was a strong smell of stale alcohol and cigarette smoke.

During this same period, and accompanied by a trainee officer, I followed the bright light of fire in the sky until we came to a caravan park in Herston, an inner city suburb of Brisbane. A caravan was well alight, and a number of people were shouting at us that there was someone still in the caravan. As I approached the screen door of the caravan, I could see the outline of man on the other side of the door. The door would not budge, locked and melted into position due to the immense heat. I tried to open the door, but after a few minutes, the figure on the other side erupted in flames and dropped to the floor. All that I could do was to find a garden hose, and lay on the ground and direct the water to neighbouring caravans and the gas bottles until the fire crew arrived. The smell and sight remained with me for a long time. Over time it faded. This was my first attendance at a critical incident. I remember preparing the statements for the coroner and giving evidence to the coroner's court. I cannot remember any support from the organisation. I can recall going to the Police Club and having a few beers. It was the mid 1980s and that was how we supported each other. We talked about it over a beer at the club. Did this sit well with me? I knew no better and I certainly could not have known that 34 years later those smells and scenes would come to the forefront of my mind.

Like many police officers, I progressed my career from uniform to the Criminal Investigation Branch (CIB) after three years in uniform. Commencing my first day in the Drug Squad, I reported for duty in a newly acquired suit and tie, to be told by the Detective Superintendent 'to take a look around sport, that clobber is for court here'. I perused the room, and I saw a group of detectives in torn jeans, t-shirts, shorts and baseball caps. Within a couple of hours, I was sitting as a new plain clothed investigator surrounded by my mentors, hardened detectives. 'So, do you smoke dope?' the Sergeant asked. 'No', I answered. 'Well you will by the time you finish here. Do you drink piss (alcohol)?' 'No, not much', I answered. 'Well, Jesus, you aren't going to last here mate, and you might want to start, otherwise no bastard here is gonna trust ya'. How could this be right? How could the very people charged with upholding the law be so cavalier with those same laws? Again, it must be the way in which to bring good to the public, one must have to think and act like the very criminals we were to catch. As a young, eager and excited plain clothes Constable 1st Class, I was challenged yet again.

In his chapter in this collection, Grant Edwards talks about his backpack. My backpack was already starting to get a few stones put into it. I spent six years in the Drug Squad, and I am proud to say that the day I left I still had not smoked dope, I did not see anyone smoke dope; I did drink a bit more than I used to, but overall, my experience was formed surrounded by hard working and ethical detectives. I moved around some other squads, and then moved in the Bureau of Criminal Intelligence. Working on covert surveillance and investigative work, security intelligence and dignitary protection and special event intelligence. This was a dream posting.

It was one afternoon shift in the office when we received a call from Police Operations to deploy to the Treasury Casino in the Brisbane Central Business District. On arrival I saw a number of the Special Emergency Response Team (SERT) members, and the Inspector-in-Charge at the door of the Casino. I had worked with him as a trainee and we remained close. As I approached he asked, 'Do you have a vest?'. I replied: 'Yeah, sure, do I need one?' He explained: 'See that briefcase, it is apparently packed with explosives'. The Casino was in lockdown, with a single man on one of the floors armed with a handgun, stating that he had placed briefcases with explosives in them that he would detonate with his mobile phone should anyone come close. SERT had the man contained and a negotiator, who I knew very well, was talking to the man. My offsider and I were to provide intelligence support for the incident. We moved to the same floor as the hostage situation, and assumed a position in an office two doors down from the hostage stronghold. We were provided access to the casino's security camera network and established communications with the forward commander and QPS systems. I placed the camera onto the mobile phone in the individual's hand, and saw a phone number which he said would detonate the devices. The number came up to a Gold Coast residence. Throughout the course of the night, I had established that the male registered to the address on the Gold Coast had recently been treated for mental health issues in Western Australia. Tracking down the psychiatrist, I was on the telephone to the psychiatrist getting strategies for dealing with the man. I moved forward to talk to the negotiator, when I heard a number of gunshots. As I looked up, I saw the man with the gun being lifted off his feet and falling to the ground. On reviewing the security cameras, I saw that he had casually turned the firearm in the direction of the SERT members and that they had shot him. The paramedics deemed the premises to be unsafe due to the briefcase devices. We provided first aid to the man. Unfortunately, he died at the scene.

I was then deployed to the Gold Coast to brief local detectives on the incident with a view to executing a search warrant on the residence. At this stage, we thought the incident had been an armed hold-up that had escalated. Around 2am in the morning, we executed the search warrant on the premises. Inside we found a woman and three young children. They were the wife and family of the man who, a few hours before, had died during a police shooting. As I was the one who had the most information, it was left to me to explain why we were there. The woman would not separate from the children, and demanded that I tell her in front of the children. After doing so, I think all five of us broke down.

After searching the premises, and going back to the local police station and preparing my statement of facts, I returned to Brisbane at about 2.30 pm. I had last briefed my Acting Inspector at 11 pm the night before, and I was then under the command and control of the Police Commander-in-Charge. The Inspector knew that I had been deployed to the Gold Coast, and knew that I was on an 8am to 4pm shift on this day. The first thing I heard when I walked back into the office, however, was the Inspector yelling at me. Why had I not sought permission for overtime? The tiredness, mixed with the evenings events, were starting to take their toll. I threw a few choice words back at the Inspector before the Superintendent approached me and suggested we went for a coffee. As we walked out the main door of the office, there was a small office on the right. This office was the Crime Operations Command's psychologist's office. As we walked past, the Superintendent pushed me in the open door and said 'he needs to talk to you'. A startled psychologist looked up, saw my dishevelled look and asked if I 'was okay?'. I abruptly advised that I was, as long as the 'so and so' Inspector found some decency. This was my first experience of how the Police Service in that period dealt with mental health and crisis debriefs. The negotiator who also worked in the Bureau had been left to her own devices after the event. She had crashed into two parked cars as she got her car out of where she had parked it, and had gone home to have a few stiff drinks. Things between 1998 and 2000 had not changed a great deal. There was no follow up with me. Admittedly, I chose not to follow up with anyone either. I simply got on with the job. I came in and did what we had to do.

I had been appointed the lead Intelligence Officer for the Commonwealth Heads of Government Meeting (CHOGM) 2001 event to be held in Brisbane. Because of this appointment I moved to Canberra in 2001, leaving the Queensland Police Service (QPS) after 16 years. My departure was a combination of two things. The first was opportunity: someone wanted me. All of a sudden, I was no longer just another number. (I recall my number today like my own birthday—6202). How had I simply become a number? The taste of that Inspector's attitude was still sour in my mouth. Notably, I had no idea why until another 16 years were to pass.

My belief system had been broken. I thought we were meant to look out for each other. We had a duty to the families to ensure we all got home safely. And yet, I had just endured a failed overtime claim. In fact, I never claimed for my duties that night. The QPS could shove their money, I thought. I remember the day that I finished my career with the QPS. I had driven the work vehicle to the office in the morning. At that time, police received free travel on public transport in Queensland. As I relinquished my badge, my constant companion because I was, like all police officers, always on duty,

I felt this tinge of sadness. The Superintendent offered to have one of the boy's drive me home. I declined his well-meaning offer. I wanted to show them that I was more than a 'copper'. I was more than Sergeant 6202. Then followed a solitary and teary walk to the Roma Street Train Station where I bought myself a one-way ticket north. I had left my police career behind. I felt empty, like a large part of who I was stayed behind in that building. It is an emptiness that remains with me. Two decades later, I still find myself talking about the 16 years I had with the Queensland Police. Why? Why is it that it is important to do that? I have had a wonderful public sector career since but still revert to those tumultuous memories.

My time in the public service has seen me work in and around law enforcement for 19 years. I initially moved to Canberra and worked in counter terrorism, mainly crisis coordination, investigations, Integrity Agency and risk and assurance. In 2016, I was performing the duties of a Chief Audit Executive and Chief Risk Officer. The role also included Integrity and Professional Standards and Department Security. I was the Secretary's principal advisor in relation to these matters. In dealing with Integrity and Professional Standards, I was responsible for interacting with people as a sanction delegate when an integrity or security investigation led to termination of employment. In each and every case, there were terrible stories of personal hardship. In each instance, the individual was no longer deemed suitable for employment in an organisation requiring high levels of trust. I personally met with each and every individual, listening to their stories. At times, it was a gut wrenching role. Sometimes other senior executives were involved. The Audit role gave me an opportunity to couple my innately inquisitive nature and professional skills, derived from policing, with my experience in the anti-corruption investigations and allowed scope to improve systems.

One particular day looms large in my memory. I recall every detail. It began when I was invited to raise an issue that had been bothering me about a departmental project. At the request of the Secretary, the meeting included several Deputy Secretaries. Some weeks later I met with the particular Deputy Secretary whose responsibilities included the project that was causing me angst. Although my role was simply to suggest improvements, the Deputy Secretary challenged my integrity and questioned my use to the organisation. As the meeting ended I left for an external meeting. I was travelling by car and became lost. I suddenly could not remember the way to a well-known

Canberra building. I was reduced to tears after the exchange that I had just endured at the hands of the Deputy Secretary. I considered my role to be important. I was doing my best to improve the department's performance. Plainly, this approach was not welcomed by one very senior officer. I remember texting both the Australian Border Force (ABF) Commissioner and the Secretary of the Department, urgently seeking a reallocation of duties. I explained the situation and declared that I was over being abused for trying to improve the department's functioning. I felt extremely sad and anxious. I recognised an intense distrust of the workplace hierarchy. My mental processes told me to 'suck it up'. I look back and now realise that both the work environment and my personal life had reached boiling point.

Away from the office my life was brimming with stress. I had placed my elderly parents into a nursing home against their wishes. The next task was cleaning their home of more than 60 years in preparation for its sale. I was also dealing with a son who attempted suicide and a daughter, who had moved away from home for university, being diagnosed with Type 1 diabetes. My personal back pack was now full. The human body is merely a vessel for the emotions. Human beings have a capacity for maintaining resilience but are not fitted with a full indicator. I was overflowing. After consultations, it was agreed that I would move into the newly formed ABF. I would be an Assistant Commissioner responsible for close support command which included the maritime unit, the detector dog program and the training college.

As I finished my duties in the Department, I became aware of what could be called 'an integrity issue' involving the then ABF Commissioner. I had known him for nearly 30 years. We had been sworn into the Queensland Police together. I dealt with these matters in what I considered an appropriate manner. I then moved into the ABF where I encountered other newly identified concerns relating to integrity and accountability. Again, I dealt with the matters at hand. Some were considered by the new Commissioner. At this point, the investigation of the previous Commissioner began. Unfortunately, as is often the case with these types of investigations, I feared being made a scapegoat. This is a continuing issue for law enforcement and integrity agencies throughout the world—the investigator is depicted as the villain.

In July 2018, as I arrived home from work after a very difficult day, I received a call from one of my Commanders as I drove my into the driveway. A deployed officer with access to firearms was considered suicidal. For over an hour we devised a strategy to remove the risk from the officer and to implement a care plan. As I walked to the front door of my home, my body started to tremble. I was powerless to stop the trembling which continued for some hours. At about 3 am, still trembling, I quietly went outside to clear my head. I was now suicidal. Never in my life had I thought of suicide. I had investigated, or been a part of investigations on behalf of the coroner, instance of suicide. I had a view, admittedly a very biased view, about people who had taken their own lives.

My wife took me to the emergency department of the local hospital where I was assessed. The medical staff recommended that I enter the psychiatric ward. Although my recollection is hazy, I think that I agreed and I became a voluntary patient for the next five weeks. By now I was extremely anxious and severely depressed. My inner state had escalated into a crisis within four hours. I had gone from being a high performer, or so I thought, to being someone of no worldly use. I was absolutely convinced that I would be a scapegoat for problems at work, that I would lose my job and find myself unable to support my family. They would, I had persuaded myself, be better off without me.

On my first day in hospital, I sent the Secretary and the Commissioner emails stating that I was sorry that I had not been able to improve the corporate hygiene of the organisation nor raise its ambient level of integrity. The email featured a frank admission: I took full responsibility for my failure. That word would be repeated in my mind over, and over, and over. Failure. I had a responsibility to the organisation. I was committed to its health and wellbeing. Simultaneously, I also felt my work was of no use. This judgement soon took on an intimate dimension: I was, therefore, of no use. After five weeks in the hospital mental health ward I was off work for another four months. My medical team suggested more time away from the office but I was very keen to return and prove my worth. I did not want to be labelled 'that guy in the corner' ... that malingerer. I wanted to show that my health difficulties were not due to the continuing integrity investigations. All of these things were scorched into my mind from policing days. I started to have flashbacks to the two critical incidents mentioned earlier. The professional caring for me believed I was suffering from an adjustment disorder and post-traumatic stress disorder (PTSD). I had heard of PTSD and thought I knew something of its causes and consequences. As a diagnosis it made sense. Every time I visited Brisbane for either personal or professional reasons, I would go to the Casino, sit at the bar, have one beer and then leave. I did not know why; I never considered it closely. It was now apparent that I was going back to the scene, to visit some unfinished business in my head that I would now learn. My PTSD is not associated with the graphic images, however. Nor is it an outcome of delivering terrible and tragic news to a family. For me, it arose from a strong distrust of senior management. It did not matter what I did, senior management found reason to criticise. I had not sought approval for the overtime. I had not kept quiet about the project going wrong. I had questioned their integrity and professionalism. In sum, I had not been able to change the culture of a whole organisation.

This mindset was cemented within a few hours of my short-term discharge from hospital one Saturday morning. The aim was to assimilate gradually back into society. My wife picked me up from hospital and drove me the short distance to our home. I opened a newspaper. On page four I was stunned by a half-page advertisement seeking applicants for ABF Assistant Commissioner positions. I told myself: this was my job. My fears were becoming a reality. I was going to lose my job. Here was affirmation: I was useless. On my half-day trip home, I lasted exactly 13 minutes before my wife returned me to the hospital. I was shaking uncontrollably and crying. Eventually I was medicated. This was, of course, a generic round calling for appointments. I would return to my previous position although it was no longer, given the state of my health, really suitable for me or the organisation. It was decided the best thing was to move into a non-operational role. This would assist my recovery. It was good for me and the ABF. But I continued to think the move was about getting rid of me. I was just a number. I could easily be discarded and just as readily replaced.

Just before Christmas that year, I was asked to attend the Secretary's office the following day. Also included in the invitation was the departmental employment lawyer. This was the same lawyer who attended the meetings that I convened with people who were about to be dismissed. I remember the tears welling in my eyes. My body was shaking and I soon left. I think I spoke to the lawyer, muttering something about not being there tomorrow. I also vividly recall being in ABF full dress uniform, standing under some trees beside the Hume Highway.

My family was far better off without me. Again, I was going to be a failure. This did not sit with who I was. I knew that I had done everything possible to ensure the integrity of the department had been improved. No one cared, or so I thought. The lawyer had realised something was wrong. She had escalated the situation to the General Counsel who then rang my mobile and texted. After about four texts, I looked at my phone. 'We love ya Stevo' was all it said. It was enough for me to snap out of my mission to end my life. Someone in the organisation cared enough to tell me that. I slowly drove home and I attended the Secretary's office the next day to be advised that I had not done anything wrong. I was not going to be a scapegoat. My ethics were suitable for the organisation.

Sometime later I was approached by the Chief Operating Officer and asked if I was interested in leading the health and child wellbeing area. I agreed because, as a senior executive, you do what is asked. I have thoroughly loved the work. I have a lived experience which I felt compelled to tell other staff via a video of my journey, in order to help at least one other person going through a difficult mental health journey.

One officer who has also experienced mental health challenges and wants to share his story is Geoffrey Lock. He received the Chief Executive Officer's bravery award for saving an individual's life while risking his personal safety, demonstrating courage in difficult circumstances and outstanding commitment and willingness to rescue and ensure the survival of an individual. Geoff was attending the super yacht *La Masquarade* in Campbells Cove Sydney during 2014 when he observed a fully clothed woman enter the water. She then proceeded to swim directly into the ferry lanes of Circular Quay in Sydney Harbour. Without hesitation, and putting himself in harms way, Geoff boarded a tender with a crew member from *La Masquarade* and pursued the woman through the ferry lane. He signalled to a number of oncoming ferries to avoid a collision. After tense negotiation with the woman he was able to persuade her to embark in the tender and return her to shore. This sounds good and the kind of day you see other officers have and ponder: will I ever have a day like that? Here's the thing: you might. But it will never conform to imagination. This story of bravery does not cover a few crucial elements, ones that might assist the reader.

Four years later, Geoff was working in a different role and in a different city. The *La Masquarade* incident came up during an ice-breaker activity on a training course. These activities are very common. It was a simple getting-to-know-you exercise based on the question: 'Have you ever saved a life. And if so, what were the circumstances.' After the ice-breaker, Geoff went back to an ordinary day and an ordinary shift. It did not really feel that different until later the same night when he tried to sleep. In his mind, as if she was present with him, the face of the woman he rescued was visible. She would not go away. Something associated with writing it down and talking about the incident had made it real. The incident now had its own personality. After that night, the experience worsened. It was disorientating, terrifying even. Geoff did not know what was going on in his mind. The onset of his PTSD was a nightmare, a waking nightmare. If it hadn't been for his wife recognising something was happening and insisting Geoff consult his doctor, he may not be alive today.

The only way Geoff thought he could deal with the legacy of this experience was to end his life. Geoff did not want to die; he just had to get away from the nightmare within his head. It is difficult, if not impossible, to imagine trying and then convincing a young woman who had thrown herself into Sydney Harbour in the middle of the busiest ferry lanes in Australian waters, that this was not her day to die? Or to imagine the thoughts of a father whose son is dangling over the side of a ship in a four metre swell, that you, on a vessel below, have that child's legs and will ensure his safety, looking into the eyes of a father who cannot speak English, and attempting to convey: 'I have got him, let him go'? Can you imagine carrying a young woman covered in excrement off a barge in the hope that her dishevelled state would save her from being raped? For some people in some professions, they can imagine these things because that is who they are and that is what they do. They train and train for things to go wrong. But what happens if they end up in the water with a child in their arms? What about the day when they need to draw, and possibly discharge, their firearm? What about when they are in Sydney Harbour, trying to pull someone from the water and they continuing resisting while a group of nearby colleagues are offering competing opinions even as a ferry rapidly draws near? It is crucial that training includes the reality of the full range of operational possibilities.

There is also another crucial element that needs to be recognised and acknowledged: it's the build-up and the culmination. Although the Sydney Harbour incident was the trigger that put Geoff into crisis, there were other events that could have had the same impact. On another occasion, Geoff was up a ladder on a container ship. He was adjacent to the second level of containers in pouring rain. He was trying to put an endoscope in the seal to check its contents and he slipped. He grabbed the edge of the container and just held on. What did Geoff do after this event? He continued with the task at hand. He counted his blessings and thought sparingly of what could have been. It is events such as these to which officers are exposed repeatedly. But there is also the build-up and the need to better address the build-up because it is the culmination of such events that create problems. To offer an analogy: when you have a broken leg, you get a care plan. Other than a small number of people who have complications, the vast majority can have confidence in their progress week by week. There are stages of progress in regaining mental health that indicate improvement but the distance between milestones will be different for every person. It is dependent on so many things: personal situations, levels of support, responses to treatment, work history and many other factors.

Geoff and I have both felt the stigma associated with making mental health admissions. The stigma is a big deal. The attitude of the law enforcement community is getting better but being told to ignore what has been seen and heard, to forget the images and the sounds, is utterly unrealistic. In fact, it is simply not possible. Some things remain and leave an indelible imprint. What will people say? Will they decide it is no more than an act? People become the focus of workplace gossip. Being on the receiving end, feeling the force of stigma, being conscious of the disbelief, is stressful in itself. When someone is off work with PTSD, they are not off having a holiday or living it up. As Geoff's experience reveals, PTSD is a full time job. It is double shifts, every day and without respite because it is happening in your head. What most people do not see are the appointments that the sufferer forces themselves to make to ensure they still receive a salary. The thought of not getting paid, facing life without money is so terrifying that the traumatised sufferer leaves the safety of their home, engages with an otherwise uncaring world, propelled to connect with everyday life with a racing heart so fast it causes chest pain. And the sufferer bears this because they want to get better, even when they suspect the treatment is making them worse. They could be embarking on this journey with little or no sleep due to nightmares. The sufferer cannot concentrate for long on anything. In this state of mind they must attend to their daily duties, make and attend appointments and balance all that comes with life, because life does not stop just because an individual stops.

Geoff was helped by the number of people who reached out to him from the 'ABF family'. He recalled: 'colleagues and ex-colleagues reaching out with texts, calls, messages ... it was amazing'. He shared another story. One Christmas Geoff did not have any money. When he answered a knock on his front door, he was greeted by two work colleagues. Inside a card was $500. Geoff's advice for anyone wanting to reach out to a colleague in crisis: a text message is perfect. I share this view. If only I had received a text message letting me know that an advertisement for new positions would appear in that day's newspapers. Geoff and I recognise the difficulty of knowing what to do. Those who are concerned want to avoid crowding their colleague—an experience that ought to be avoided. So a simple text message to be digested when the person in crisis is in the right frame of mind to deal with external contact is likely to assist. These gestures will align with the individual's core values. Outreach of this kind will enable a person to stay with an organisation because they will continue to feel connected to its cause.

I have felt compelled personally and professionally to break the stigma associated with mental health in law enforcement agencies. It has become a calling. It was not, however, my idea. Grant Edwards led a similar movement in the Australian Federal Police (AFP) a few years earlier. It was the right thing to do. Since then, I have enthusiastically embraced a role within the Health Services Division. For me, it is the perfect blend of a lived experience, new knowledge of mental health issues, and a position sufficiently senior in the organisation to make a difference. It also allows me to contribute directly to the personal wellbeing of my colleagues. This role takes me back to why I joined the police and why the members of the New South Wales Police Rescue Squad are committed to the safety and security of others.

My present role is best described as a calling. As I continue to deliver presentations on mental health in the workplace and advocate for changes to the conditions under which people work with a strong focus on prevention, I am becoming well again. While PTSD and wariness of senior management gain momentum from time to time, I am grateful for an understanding boss. By and large, I am strong. I have aligned my core values with the work I undertake. I cannot think of a time when I have been happier in my employment. There are still bad days but they are not without meaning. There are plenty of people who go to work every day with the intention of making life better for others. That is why they may have decided upon a law enforcement career. It is about giving to the public and willingly becoming their servant.

5   Organisational culture and leadership: their influence on police wellbeing

Grant Edwards

'The ordinary response to atrocities is to banish them from the consciousness. Certain violations of the social compact are too terrible to utter aloud: this is the meaning of the word unspeakable'.

Judith Lewis Herman, *Trauma and Recovery: The Aftermath of Violence— From Domestic Abuse to Political Terror*

*T*he concept of wellness within the policing workplace is relatively new with many organisations actively pursuing programs to improve the lives of their staff. The exposure of police to continual trauma is sufficient justification to focus on the widespread prevalence of mental illness among the policing community. More than ever police are succumbing to the accumulated stress of frequent exposure to the horrors of their job. Combined with stresses in their private lives these sources of tension increase several risks in terms of their psychological and physical health, their family relationships, physical injuries, emotional trauma and ambiguity and negativity about their roles and function in society.

This chapter focuses on the psychological element of wellness and how police organisational culture and leadership influences and impacts police wellbeing. I will draw on my personal lived mental health experience as an Australian Federal Police (AFP) member to accentuate this conversation with a view to identifying and influencing change.

The impact of mental health on society and policing

'Trauma is hell on earth. Trauma resolved is a gift from the gods.'
Peter A Levine

Mental disorders are on the rise and will cost the global economy $16 trillion (USD) by 2030, according to the 2018 Lancet Commission, with an estimated 12 billion working days lost every year (LaMontagne, et al 2016). In Australia, mental health conditions are costing approximately $12 billion annually. One in five (20 percent) Australians aged 16–85 experience a mental illness in any year. Almost half (45 percent) of all Australians will experience a mental illness in their lifetime. At least six Australians die from suicide and a further thirty people will attempt to take their own life every day. Men are at greatest risk of suicide but least likely to seek help. In 2011, men accounted for over three-quarters (76 percent) of deaths from suicide (Australian Budget 2017).

It is well known that police suffer a higher prevalence of stress-related illnesses than the general public (Soomro & Yanos. 2018) due to the hazardous and stressful nature of their occupation (Axelrod 2019; Burke 2016; Deschamps et al. 2003; Tuckey et al. 2012). Large numbers of police continue to take their lives by suicide (Schwartz 2017) and many more remain reluctant to acknowledge and present operational stress injuries (Miller 2005, Carleton et al. 2018). Police executives around the world are struggling with how best to develop and implement programs within their organisations to successfully support the mental health of their personnel (Whitley 2020).

A 2017 study conducted by researchers at the University of Toronto in Canada demonstrated the dangers of failing to acknowledge and deal with mental health among police. Researchers interviews found that first responders with mental health injuries exhibited 'performance deficits on complex cognitive tasks', which could include tasks that required first responders to assess risks, and plan multi-step responses to an emergency, especially complex operations where there are multiple offenders and or victims (Regehr & LeBlanc, 2017). The risk to society is high if these health issues are not dealt with appropriately.

A 2018 Cambridge University study of police in the United Kingdom revealed two-thirds of all respondents said they had a mental health issue directly resulting from police work. Yet, almost all the survey's respondents—some 93 percent—said they would go to work as usual if suffering from psychological issues such as stress or depression. They would do so without seeking treatment due to the associated negative organisational and leadership influences (Hargreaves et al. 2018).

The complexities of being a police officer

'I know what it's like to be afraid of your own mind'.
Unknown

There are so many positives of being a police officer, being able to help and contribute to your society and serve your community and country. Having the opportunity of saving lives, taking the worst criminals, like murderers and rapists, off the streets; ensuring child sex offenders are bought to justice; taking huge quantities of drugs out of the community and helping developing societies or those post-conflict nations to enable peace and security—just to name a few.

Policing is one of the most rewarding careers someone can have. It is often referred to as a noble calling (Covey 2020):

> It has always been my firm belief that policing is one of …. (the) most noble of professions. The actions of any police officer, in an instant, can impact an individual for life, and even a community for generations. Given this realisation, every police officer must be centered on what is important. Service, justice, and fundamental fairness, these are the foundational principles in which every police action must be grounded.

Many police officers will tell you it is not a job or a career but a way of life; how they view the world, how they assess people, where they sit in public places, constantly scanning locations and people, being suspicious and distrustful of others and hyper-vigilant about the safety and security of loved ones. Essentially, many officers will define themselves by their job and it comes to assume their identity and the sense of whom they are (Subošić et al. 2018) given the '24/7' expectation of being 'on duty'.

Policing is also one of the toughest and most dangerous career choices you could embark upon. After all, what other profession requires you to continually deal with the worst of humanity? What other job causes you to be in a constant state of hyper-vigilance, yet at the same time remain calm enough to be a counsellor, a social worker, a psychologist, a medic, a lawyer, a teacher or a prison warden? What other profession authorises you to take a person's liberty, or, at worse, execute deadly force on another human being, but then mandates that you render assistance to the person who has just tried to harm or kill you? What job causes you to wonder whether you will come home to your loved ones at the end of your shift each day (MacDonald 2016).

Most people do not call upon a police officer when everything is conventional; people call when the situation is beyond their control. Over a career it is not unreasonable to expect police to be exposed to more than 250 traumatic events (Heyman et al 2018). Yet, police fail to recognise how what they see, hear, smell, taste and feel affects them daily (Kates 2015).

As first responders we wear that facade of being unbreakable, of being that rock for everyone, and we forget to take care of ourselves. We do not deal with the cracks or the seeds that find their way in. As the pressure inside builds we either become accustomed to it or choose not to see and deal with it. Usually, it is not until it is too late that we see and feel it, and we break. As a law enforcement colleague once remarked:

> It's like the day you join you're given a backpack and every day you go to work you add a little pebble. After 10 years the backpack has gotten considerably heavier, but you carry on, as you are still young and fit. After 20 years the number of little pebbles has increased and the backpack is substantially heavier. You can only carry it for some of the time, the rest you have to drag it. After 30 years you can hardly move the backpack. It's so heavy that you are physically, mentally and emotionally drained from having to move it, the pain is just too much and the commitment, motivation and vigour you once possessed has all but been drained from your body.

The stressors of policing

'We do not heal in isolation, but in community'.
    S Kelley Harrell, *Gift of the Dreamtime—Reader's Companion*

Our societies are hugely dependent upon the policing institution, the energy of its members, and critical decision-making skills (Edwards et.al. 2020). Left untreated, mental illness considerably impacts these capacities and is costly to society (Karaffa & Koch 2015, Heyman et al. 2018). It is well known that mental illness is treatable and yet, without treatment, the affected police officer is severely limited in their function. Further, and perhaps most importantly, this potentially places the community at risk. (Heffren & Hausdorf 2016).

Although exposure to trauma has been rightly declared the main reason for operational stress injuries (Tuckey et al. 2012), it has equally been argued that psychological illness in policing has more to do with the impact organisational culture, leadership style and attitudes has on mental health than the traumatic nature of the job itself (Deschênes et al. 2018, Edwards and Kotera 2020).

Irrespective of rank, position, role and function internal stressors in policing can be just as damaging to members as traumatic ones and there are many, almost all of which can induce an injury response:

- *Internal stressors*—those originating within the organisation, poor supervision and leadership, absence of career development opportunities, inadequate reward system, offensive policies, over reporting and paperwork, budgetary constraints and austerity measures
- *External stressors*—jurisdictional isolation, seemingly ineffective legal and court systems, adverse media accounts, impact of social media / media, derogatory remarks and adverse government interference, external oversight entities, insurance provider hostility
- *Performance stressors*—role conflict, adverse work schedules, fear and danger, sense of uselessness, and absence of closure
- *Individual stressors*—feeling overcome by fear and danger, pressures to conform, gender disparity, bullying, sexual harassment, Detective vs Uniform, sworn v unsworn, city vs remote policing, member ethnicity and cultural differences, lack of LGBQTI understanding, perceived specialist group superiority
- *Social Isolation Stressors*—cynicism, isolation, and alienation from the community; prejudice and discrimination
- *Organisational stressors*—administrative philosophy, changing of policies and procedures, morale, job satisfaction, bullying, harassment and misdirected performance measures
- *Functional stressors*—role conflict / confusion, use of discretion, and legal mandates
- *Personal stressors*—off duty life, including family, illness, problems with children and aging parents, marital distress and financial constraints

- *Physiological stressors*—fatigue, medical conditions, and shift work effects

- *Psychological stressors*—all the above plus the exposure to repulsive situations (Subošić et al. 2018, Police Stressors 2011).

It is also acknowledged that added pressures in law enforcement elevates officers' risks of experiencing co-morbid physical manifestations like high blood pressure, insomnia, increased levels of destructive stress hormones and heart related problems which take their toll on police, especially post retirement (Violanti, J. etal 2013).

A personal journey

'I'm not faking being sick. I'm actually faking being well'.
Unknown

My 34 years of experience in the Australian Federal Police has revealed that the public perceive police to be something other than human, expected to accept and tolerate things well beyond that of anyone else in society. We are mums, dads, brothers, sisters, sons and daughters. Beyond the badge we are netball, cricket, soccer or football coaches. We volunteer in our communities, whether it be Surf Lifesaving, Rural Fire Service or as St John's Ambulance officers. We feel pain, we cry, we bleed just like the rest of society does. We often have to do things that run against our moral compass in enforcing the law, but that is what we take an oath to do. The main difference, however, is we are human beings dealing with inhumane things.

Constant exposure to crime causes us to behave differently to the rest of society. We rarely like to reside where we work. We like to sit in the back corner when at restaurants or unfamiliar places, so our backs are covered. We look for exit points in movie theatres and shopping centres in case the worst-case scenario presents. We are constantly scanning, looking for potential threats. We do not tend to associate with the broader community, preferring to instead socialise with likeminded others or keep to ourselves. Most of all we are forever sceptical and untrusting. It is the way we trained.

The reality of being a police officer is often, however, quite different from the images portrayed through the media and entertainment industry. The profession has been a constant source of interest, whether it be in the latest form of a crime novel, television show or a movie. Just think how many are produced for consumption each and every year. As ratings would suggest, it seems the public are highly attracted to the perverse nature of society and accompanying underlying criminality.

Joining the AFP was one of the most important days of my life. I could not wait to take criminals off the streets. I went to work each and every day to make a difference, to do something positive, and I loved my job. From the time I entered the academy as a fresh-faced recruit I was taught elements of the law, internal procedures, protocols, drill, physical self-defence and emergency driving. I was prepared and trained to use batons, capsicum spray, handcuffs and the use of lethal force. I was bought to the peak of physical fitness, skilled and educated in how to maintain neutrality with my emotions and to remain composed and calm in situations where others would not. I was shaped to distrust and question everything which would be so pervasive it would eventually permeate all facets of my work and personal life. What I was not taught or exposed to was how to deal with the stress and trauma I would experience throughout my career. How do you prepare someone to experience human tragedy? There was nothing that would quite prepare me for the sights, smells and sounds that you encounter as a police officer. How do you explain to a new recruit that over the course of his or her lifetime they will experience these traumatic events?

Throughout a policing career it is not unreasonable to expect to be verbally abused, physically assaulted, spat upon, bitten, have urine or some other bodily fluid thrown at you. You will suffer physical injuries, cuts, abrasions, sprains and broken bones. You may deal with horrendous things such as homicides, rapes, assaults, fatal motor vehicle accidents; seeing another human being beheaded; or the horrendous impact of chemical weapons used on young innocent children in a conflict zone. You could experience the devastation and catastrophe of natural disasters.

You will remove children from their home who are suffering welts and sores from a flea-infested, maggot-riddled household where the filth and stench permeates every element of your senses. You could be present in a surgical theatre alongside doctors trying to save the life of a drug courier who had swallowed pellets containing drugs, or dealing with the body of a drug overdose victim whose 'friends' were so drugged that they used the chord off an iron in an attempt to electrically jump-start his heart. You may experience children who are sexually assaulted and violently molested, some as young as six months of age, abused and filmed for distribution over the internet, listening to their distraught screams, their sobs, their distressed pleas begging for the abuse to stop.

You may be deployed overseas to hostile environments where you are vigorously removed from a vehicle at gunpoint by the local military and threatened, or be attacked by Taliban insurgents in Afghanistan who detonate their bomb vests and indiscriminately shoot at anyone or anything that moves. You may be exposed to debilitating and life threatening diseases like Tick paralysis, MERS, Chikungunya, Dengue Fever, Blastocystis and Schistomasiasis.

The public will monitor and film your every move by mobile devices and selectively post elements that will be scrutinised, assessed and adjudicated on popular digital media sites without the full and truthful context being portrayed. When you get to court you will be questioned at length by defence lawyers and have your integrity, professionalism and credibility attacked. In some cases, you are ridiculed, patronised and mocked before your peers, the jury and the legal profession without any opportunity for rebuttal.

Worst of all, criminals will physically and psychologically threaten and intimidate you and your family. You will work incessant hours, develop poor sleeping and nutritional habits, cease physical activities, form a reliance on alcohol and medications and withdraw from family and loved ones. You will miss many Christmases, birthdays, significant family events, your children's milestone events, be away from family and the home for extended periods, isolate yourself, become angry and intolerant, cry and sob and eventually suffer exhaustion.

You will encounter good and bad leaders, suffer indignation because of poor management with at times toxic and inconsistent leadership and supervision impacting you substantially. You may potentially be bullied and unnecessarily harassed. You will attend far too many unnecessary funerals of colleagues. This is not an exhaustive list, but these examples are all personal experiences. Many others in the policing profession have suffered and been exposed to far worse.

Policing taught me not to trust anyone, my work colleagues, friends, not even my family. I was sceptical and was not sure where to go and did not know who was there for me. I had become physically and mentally exhausted and the 'brain fog' so severe that I no longer had the will to fight the demons inside my head. Early in 2014, following my return from Afghanistan, a sinister thought occurred. The voice inside my head would assure me the misery I was battling could be ended by committing suicide. I was internally tortured by the thoughts, but I would eventually commence meticulously planning my own suicide. I had progressed to executing it—but thankfully one thought kept pushing me not to. That thought was the feelings of pain, abandonment, anger and weight that accompanied the suicide of my grandfather and the profound impact his death had on me as a 10 year old. I chose not to put my loved ones through the same.

Throughout life I had the courage to take on some of the toughest roles as a police officer. But I could not muster the courage to declare I was mentally hurting. I did my utmost to protect our broader community, but without realising it, the stress and trauma of my job ate away at me until I was left psychologically vulnerable and exposed. While I used my smile as a mask, my relentless fight to preserve my job took every ounce of energy from me. The policing culture had revealed to me that declaring a mental health issue to my superiors in my mind was a career killer.

Lessons learnt

'You are not broken and in need of fixing. You are wounded and in need of healing'.
Danu Morrigan

Police culture is an extremely powerful component of the profession which directly and indirectly impacts every police employee, whether sworn or unsworn (Brough, et al 2016, Subošić et al 2018). It contains a series of assumptions, beliefs, expectations, and philosophy that governs the profession's interactions, performance, and role (Loftus 2009). It informs police how to go about their tasks, how hard to work, what kinds of relationships to have with their fellow officers and other categories of people with whom they interact, and how they should feel about police executive, judges, laws and the requirements and restrictions they pose (Bullock & Garland 2018). It is widely perceived within police culture that acknowledging a mental health injury is a sign of weakness, a 'career killer', and places individuals into a stereotypical group, consequently leading to discrimination, isolation and alienation (Edwards & Kotera 2020).

Policing culture is a pervasive microcosm in which a closed mini-society perpetuates a sense of strong cohesion, a code of silence and secrecy, and dependence upon one another for survival. It values strength, integrity, stoicism, distrust, and self-reliance; controlled emotions, and the ability to handle complex problems (Garbarino et al 2013., Bell & Eski, 2016). These values discourage help-seeking behaviour (Stuart 2017) and impede potential disclosure of mental health injuries.

As a cop there is an awful sense of having 'lost control' by needing to ask someone else to help fix the problem; especially when they are perceived by the community to be stoic, strong, unflappable, and unshakable (Kotera et al 2018b, Soomro & Yanos 2018). Historically, the strong masculine policing culture dictated the best way to deal with stress and trauma is to undertake 'an informal debriefing session' (Brough et al 2016). This session involved only the closest of colleagues, copious quantities of alcohol and sometimes risky behaviour (Edwards & Kotera 2020). Although initially welcomed by many, this informal process only succeeded in momentarily dulling your feelings without addressing any underlying deep-rooted psychological issues. Fearful of being perceived as weak and untrustworthy, to suffer potential sanctions or loss of professional opportunities, officers are therefore unlikely to reach out and seek help, even privately.

Many police remain unwilling to declare a mental health injury. Doing so, they think, will effectively end their career. Instead, they believe their only option is living in silence and continuing to suffer alone. The cumulative and vicarious exposure to consistent trauma in law enforcement accompanied by the day-to-day social stressors that we face as humans can lead to a cocktail of mental and physical ill-health, and in many cases police will suffer from a co-morbidity of both physical and mental health degradation.

Mental health leadership is obscure, subjective, and messy to engage—uncomfortable, complex and at times highly threatening, hence the reluctance for many organisations to involve themselves in the leadership process (Heffren & Hausdorf 2016). Books, articles, podcasts on nearly every aspect of leadership crowd the management section in bookstores and online websites. In my judgement, few of these publications deal with the capacity of leaders to support mental health in the workplace. Nothing prepares a leader for how to respond when a team member quietly talks about being swept away in a wave of depression or anxiety. Leaders play a pivotal role in creating the type of environment that promotes mental and emotional well-being and in making it safe to discuss the topic in the workplace. The social, physical and policy environments within the workplace can all influence the ability or probability of individuals engaging in a better mental health program (Williams 2018).

If the build-up of stress manifests itself in physical ways, we know how to seek help. Few of us have trouble asking to go home with a migraine or if we have the flu. But when it comes to talking about burn-out, depression, or anxiety, we are hesitant to broach the topic with our friends and colleagues, let alone with those in charge of our careers. This leaves us feeling alone with our struggles and delays or prevents us from wanting or feeling able to seek help.

What can be done?

'Often it is not the initiating trauma that creates seemingly insurmountable pain, but the lack of support after'.
S Kelley Harrell

It is difficult to change human behaviour, particularly in an environment that in most cases does not encourage change (Hargreaves et al. 2018). As a leader seeking to engender understanding and support for wellness in policing, authenticity is the greatest asset. Appreciating and acknowledging that mental health problems are becoming more common in the workplace will help normalise and demystify the mental health stigma.

Stigma is considered a mark of disgrace that sets a person apart from others. When a person is labelled by their illness they are no longer seen as an individual but as part of a stereotyped group. A more sympathetic culture for those suffering from stress and mental health issues and removing the 'suck it up princess' attitude will go a long way in supporting this. By being courageous enough to be open about their own ordeals, they are making it safer for others to share their stories. By doing so it helps flip the paradigm that coming forward and seeking help for a mental health issue is not a sign of weakness, but rather a sign of strength (Long 2019). Stigma is the most significant barrier to better mental health. It requires leaders to stop pretending that they have it together all the time, to share their personal experiences, confusion, and despair they themselves may feel at times, to humanise themselves and show that it is ok to show vulnerability.

In order to engender the trust and confidence of their staff, it is important that leaders possess a basic understanding of the range of all mental health presentations, just as they would physical injuries and not just focus on PTSD and suicide. Specifically, leaders should have an appreciation of the variety of trauma and operational stress issues that regularly confront police. They include:

- *Acute trauma*—often associated with a single event that happens in one's life
- *Cumulative trauma*—adversity as indexed by a count of lifetime exposure to a wide array of potentially traumatic events
- *Compassion fatigue*—is a condition characterised by a gradual lessening of compassion over time. The condition is common among workers who work directly with victims of trauma
- *Vicarious trauma*—is a transformation from empathic engagement with traumatised people and their reports of traumatic experiences
- *Operational Stress Injury*—any persistent psychological difficulty resulting from operational duties
- *Job stress*—defined as the harmful physical and emotional responses that occur when the requirements of the job do not match the capabilities, resources, or needs of the worker
- *Moral injury*—emphasises the psychological, social, cultural, and spiritual aspects of trauma. Moral injury is a normal human response to an abnormal traumatic event where police have witnessed or been involved in matters that transgressed their deeply held moral beliefs and expectations. Moral injury can also be experienced by police who have been transgressed against in the workplace. The injury may in those cases include a sense of betrayal and anger. Those who have seen and experienced death, mayhem, destruction, and violence and have had their worldviews shattered. (Grohol, J., 2020)

Overcoming the stigma attached to mental health in policing, reducing distrust, defeating cynicism and encouraging help seeking behaviour can occur when culture and leadership are operationalised throughout institutions. Elements that may assist include:

- Attention to psychological health must form a key component of any police department's strategic objectives
- Better mental health should be normalised throughout all police vernacular, policy, governance and frameworks

- Every mental health problem regardless of cause or situation is addressed
- Mental health planning and engagement involves the basis of trust, including commitment and overt actions
- Structures designed and implemented to normalise mental health and operational stress injuries throughout the policing nomenclature
- Normalise mental health through inclusion in operational plans—search warrant affidavits, standard tactical plans, risk identification and reduction plans
- Introduce the potential risk of contracting an operational stress injury into the policing ecosystem, from pre recruit, to recruit, through to retirement and beyond
- Develop a consistent and regular communication strategy aimed at normalising mental health injuries from top down to bottom up, especially via the power of storytelling
- Focus on implementing and enhancing leadership education, understanding and training in mental health
- Mental health elements should be tied to every members' annual personal development and performance program, or similar
- Mental health scenarios and training ought to accompany annual departmental use of force and first aid training
- Development of a mental health early warning flag system for internal affairs and professional standards and ethical command areas to assist with early identification and intervention of behavioural change that may indicate a psychological injury
- Introduction of a family and loved one's program or portal as an early identification and intervention ability as it is often loved ones who first identify subtle changes in behaviour and stress levels
- Undertake unity of effort across all facets of organisational enabling services to encourage seamless interactions and communication across silos
- Encourage collaboration and partnerships among all policing agencies, support agencies and academia
- Develop and implement a consistent national standard of mental health policy and standards.

Conclusion

'The brave men and women, who serve their country and as a result, live constantly with the war inside them, exist in a world of chaos. But the turmoil they experience is not who they are'.
Robert Koger

The degradation of mental health across the globe and especially policing is a worldwide concern. The financial cost is substantial but the human cost is more concerning. Addressing police culture and leadership as a major impediment to better wellbeing in policing agencies is difficult, problematic, yet essential. Recognising, normalising and accepting that psychological injuries, just like physical injuries form an integral and expected element of policing will go a long way in assisting and encouraging members to come forward and present should they suffer any form of psychological injury. For decades I refused to acknowledge and accept that I was suffering a psychological injury. Even as I slid into the depths of my post-traumatic stress injury I stoically fought to deny or acknowledge I was even injured. The fear in doing so, in my mind meant I was weak, inferior, embarrassed and would be unable to meet my professional requirements. I would put myself in the position of believing the only way out would be through suicide.

Inculcating mental health discourse into policing throughout all facets of the policing ecosystem, nomenclature, leadership, training and culture will have a positive effect in achieving structural trust and overcoming individual scepticism. Overtly introducing constructive changes within organisations will emphasise to staff that police leaders are serious and committed to ensuring that the psychological health and wellbeing of their people is of paramount importance. By doing so, police departments will encounter greater productivity, lower levels of absenteeism, save on insurance premiums, reduce risk factors for diseases and illnesses, improve quality of life and sense of wellbeing, create a dynamic position for greater staff recruitment and retention, provide better cognitive performance, and reduced stress, and encourage and support stronger employee-employer relationships.

References

Australian Budget 2017 https://www.ag.gov.au/Publications/Budgets/Budget2017-18/Documents/PBS-AFP-2017–18.pdf.

Axelrod, T., (2019), New York police commissioner declares 'mental health crisis' after 3 officer suicides. https://thehill.com/blogs/blog-briefing-room/

news/448735-new-york-police-commissioner-declares-mental-health-crisis—retrieved 19 May 2020.

Bell, S., & Eski, Y, (2016). 'Break a leg—it's all in the mind': police officers' attitudes towards colleagues with mental health issues. *Policing*, 10(2), 95–101.

Brough, P., Chataway, S., & Biggs, A. (2016). 'You do not want people knowing you're a copper!' A contemporary assessment of police organisational culture. *International Journal of Police Science & Management*, 18(1), 28–36. DOI: 10.1177/1461355716638361.

Bullock, K., & Garland, J, (2018). Police officers, mental (ill-)health and spoiled identity. *Criminology & Criminal Justice*, 18(2), 173–189.

Burke. R. J., (ed) (2016) *Stress in Policing: Sources, consequences and interventions*. Routledge, London.

Carleton, N. R., Afifi, T. O., Turner, S., Taillieu, T., LeBouthillier, D. M., Duranceau, C., et al. (2018). "Suicidal ideation, plans, and attempts among public safety personnel in Canada". *Canadian Psychology*, 59(3), 220–231. https://doi.org/10.1037/cap0000136.

Covey, F., The Nobility of Policing-Building public trust in law enforcement from the inside out. https://www.franklincovey.com/Solutions/government/policing-trust.html. Retrieved 28 May 2020.

Deschamps, F., Paganon-Badinier, I., Marchand, A. C., & Merle, C., (2003). Sources and assessment of occupational stress in the police. *Journal of Occupational Health*, 45(6), 358–364.

Deschênes, A.-A., Desjardins, C., & Dussault, M., (2018). Psychosocial factors linked to the occupational psychological health of police officers: preliminary study. *Cogent Psychology*, 5(1), 1426271.

Edwards, A., Kotera, Y., Mental Health in the UK Police Force: a Qualitative Investigation into the Stigma with Mental Illness. *Int J Mental Health Addiction* (2020). https://doi.org/10.1007/s11469-019-00214-x.

Garbarino, S., Cuomo, G., Chiorri, C., & Magnavita, N., (2013). Association of work-related stress with mental health problems in a special police force unit. *BMJ Open*, 3(7).

Hargreaves, J., Husband, H., & Linehan, C., (2018). Police workforce, England and Wales, 31 March 2018. *Statistical Bulletin*, 11(18).

Heffren, C. D. J., & Hausdorf, P. A., (2016). Post-traumatic effects in policing: perceptions, stigmas and help seeking behaviours. *Police Practice and Research*, 17(5), 420–433.

Heyman, M., et al, (2018) The Ruderman White Paper on Mental Health and Suicide of First Responders. https://issuu.com/rudermanfoundation/docs/first_responder_white_paper_final_ac270d530f8bfb.

Karaffa, K. M., & Koch, J. M., (2015). Stigma, pluralistic ignorance, and attitudes toward seeking mental health services among police officers. *Criminal Justice and Behavior*, 43(6), 759–777.

Kates, A., (2015), *Cope Shock. Surviving Posttraumatic Stress Disorder*. Holbrook Street Press, Arizona.

Kotera, Y., Green, P., & Sheffield, D., (2018b). Mental health attitudes, self-criticism, compassion and role identity among UK Social Work Students. *The British Journal of Social Work*, 49(2), 351–370.

Loftus, B., (2009). *Police Culture in a Changing World*; Clarendon studies in criminology Oxford University Press. ISBN 0199560900, 9780199560905.

LaMontagne, A. D., Martin, A., Page, K. M., Reavley, N. J., Noblet, A. J., Milner, A. J., et al., (2014). Workplace mental health: developing an integrated intervention approach. *BMC Psychiatry*, 14(1), 131.

Long, K., (2019). Addressing the Mental Health Stigma in Law Enforcement. https://inpublicsafety.com/2019/05/addressing-the-mental-health-stigma-in-law-enforcement/. Accessed 29 May 2020.

MacDonald, H,. (2016). *The War on Cops*. Encounter Books. New York.

Miller, L. (2005). Police officer suicide: causes, prevention, and practical intervention strategies. *International Journal of Emergency Mental Health*, 7(2), 101.

Police Stressors (2011). http://www.policeptsd.com/2011/03/08/police-stressors/ accessed 1 June 2020.

Regehr, C., & LeBlanc, V. R., (2017). PTSD, acute stress, performance and decision-making in emergency service workers. *Journal of the American Academy of Psychiatry and the Law*, 45(2), 184–192. doi: 10.1037/t12199-000.

Schwartz, B. A., (2017) Living with the Sacrifice. Emotional wellness and suicide prevention for police officers Aug 18, 2017—https://www.policeone.com/health-fitness/articles/411141006-Emotional-wellness-and-suicide-prevention-for-police-officers/.

Soomro, S., & Yanos, P. T., (2018). Predictors of mental health stigma among police officers: the role of trauma and PTSD. *Journal of Police and Criminal Psychology*, 1–9.

Stuart, H., (2017). Mental illness stigma expressed by police to police. Israel Journal of Psychiatry and Related Sciences, 54(1), 18–23.

Subošić, D., Slaviša, K., & Luknar, I., (2018) Police Subculture and Potential Stress Risks. UDK:351.74–051:159.944.4.

Grohol, J., (2020) Symptoms & Treatments of Mental Disorders. https://psychcentral.com/disorders/. Accessed 28 May 2020.

The Lancet Commission on global mental health and sustainable development (2018). *The Lancet*, Vol. 392, No. 10157. (October 10).

Tuckey, M. R., Winwood, P. C., & Dollard, M. F., (2012). Psychosocial culture and pathways to psychological injury within policing. *Police Practice and Research*, 13(3), 224–240.

Violanti, J. et al, (2013). Impact Of Stress On Police Officers' Physical And Mental Health, *Science Daily*, 29 September 2008, University Bufflo. Buffalo?.

Whitley, R., (2020) The Mental Health of Police: Hope, Support, and Recovery Breaking the stigma and silence about mental distress and suicidality in police. Posted 7 April 2020. https://www.psychologytoday.com/us/blog/talking-about-men/202004/the-mental-health-police-hope-support-and-recovery—retrieved 19 May 2020.

6 Police leadership and moral wellbeing

Graham Ashton

There have been few issues as important to the law enforcement and security sector over recent years as the mental health of its employees. When using the term recent years, I would note that it has only really been over the past five years that these issues have been publicly discussed or 'surfaced' within agencies. They have, however, been in existence for many decades.

Throughout my 40 year career in law enforcement, I have seen poor mental health affect a substantial number of police officers and support staff. Many in policing are working each day under the shadow of low confidence, poor self-esteem and an overall fear in regard to their health and safety. Some choose to leave their career, and they do so with an uncertain future. This is due to untreated or poorly managed mental health issues, or both. What is also unclear to them, and is rarely articulated, is the moral injury that they may have suffered. This occurs where a person's set of values has, in their view, disconnected from the values of the organisation by which they are employed.

Beyond the legal frameworks of employment, the question remains as to what 'moral' obligation exists for policing and security agencies to provide both preventative and responsive programs of mental health and wellbeing support to employees? And further, does that obligation extend to past serving police? To be clear at the outset, the term 'moral', I consider, is generally to be concerned with that which is right and wrong, with a focus on the right. While these may be complex ethical concepts from an employer perspective, if asked the question: is it right to ensure the workplace risk of mental health injury is prevented and treated? And if a member is injured:

is it right to extend that obligation to those that leave your employment? The answer to both questions is yes. A moral obligation does exist. I would suggest that in most organisations that obligation is not conveyed in moral terms to the employee.

Policing is a field within which people generally seek to ensure alignment of their values with those of the organisation. That has certainly been the case in my own 40-year career in law enforcement. This makes the organisation's espoused values vitally important. Stated organisational values tend to be oriented towards what behaviours or traits are expected of employees. In the context of a moral contract with an employee, those values should perhaps be balanced with an articulation of the obligations of the employer as well. There are also, of course, the unstated values that exist in organisations. When these unstated values differ widely from that of an employee's stated values, then an unhealthy moral tension can exist. I think that this has occurred in regard to mental health in policing. The employee has seen it as an issue and has considered the employer obligation, but has been left feeling unsupported when the organisation remains silent in real and policy terms.

Relative to employee mental health, I have thought about this moral obligation or 'right thing', for probably eight years now. I have had good friends take their own lives as a consequence of poor mental health. I have little doubt that workplace factors were present on each occasion. Each time I have asked myself whether I could have done anything to be more responsive or attentive to the needs of these people. As organisational governance became a larger part of my role as a senior member of police, that question transitioned to challenging the obligation of the employer to ensure that these people – my colleagues – did not reach such a desperate situation in the first place.

My opportunity to make a difference became clearer when I was appointed the twenty-second Chief Commissioner of Victoria Police (CCP) on 1 July 2015. Victoria Police is a large force of more than 22,000 staff delivering 24-hour services across the state. Prior to taking up the role I naturally gave thought to the strategic direction in which the force was heading and where I could take it, as its leader. One of the key priorities I identified was employee mental health. I saw my appointment as an opportunity to place mental health and safety high on the agenda and communicate to all employees that their mental health was important to us, the organisation's leaders. This would help create alignment between the organisation's values and those of the employee. At my first press conference as CCP I outlined the need to focus on the safety of our staff and particularly their mental health. I stated that I wanted to make a difference in an area I had long been passionate about; to reduce the stigma associated with seeking support; and change decades of entrenched culture. It was a culture that regarded mental health injury as a 'weakness' not an injury.

I commenced dealing with this challenge by doing what all good managers do when they know there is a problem but lack the expertise to know what the solution looks like—I commissioned a review. I am grateful to the late Peter Cotton and his impressive team for completing a thorough examination of mental health injury and our response mechanisms. The public report that they produced was the first of its kind in Australia and was released in May 2016. Told through the lens of the injured and their families, it painted a picture of a system in dire need of attention. Victoria Police was told that our initial critical incident response was well modelled and intentioned, but badly underfunded. Injury prevention was poor, again due to inadequate funding. And, stigmatising those who declared themselves as mentally unwell or injured happened frequently. Importantly, it also identified a moral obligation to support past serving police who were in need and the report made recommendations to improve all of these areas. Now, we had a roadmap.

The case for change had been made and a willingness existed within the Command team of Victoria Police to make that change. This chapter, however, does not concern itself with the details of that work. Rather it is focussed on the moral leadership responsibilities that I had, as Chief Commissioner at that time. I found a particular opportunity to discharge that obligation in 2017. It had been a very busy year in the role, and I was tired. Without realising, I had ceased to maintain the resilience mechanisms I had subconsciously relied upon for many years. Hobbies had stopped, friends went uncontacted, exercise ceased, family events were missed. My focus on anything but work was brief. The result of this behaviour was that at the end of 2017 I was physically and mentally exhausted. Even getting up and going to work in the morning had become very difficult. My initial response was to take a short two-week period of recreation leave thinking this would fix my 'tiredness'. It did not. My trips to the local doctor yielded no real answers. I already knew I had a pre-existing medical condition that left me open to fatigue but, beyond that, physical test results gave no clear pathway. I recall a sense of hopelessness upon leaving the doctor's surgery on one occasion. I had a mountain of work obligations which I did not feel well enough to deal with. At this point, I was not sure what to do.

It became gradually clear to me that I needed to take a longer period of rest than that I had planned. I had plenty of sick leave owing, but taking it would raise many awkward questions within the force. Also, in such a public facing role, questions would be raised by the community as well. I was owed substantial recreation leave and I considered the option of taking that type of leave instead of sick leave as a means of avoiding questions. It was near Christmas, extended leave would appear usual if accompanied by the right narrative. Time needed with family came to mind as one of those narratives.

Therein lay my moral leadership dilemma. The moral obligation I had, as I saw it, needed to be considered. I had commissioned the Victoria Police mental health review and publicly committed myself to implementing its recommendations. I had for many months been travelling around Victoria exhorting staff to speak up and seek assistance. I had started to see the early signs that the negative stigma associated – positive examples started to become more usual. It was more than obvious to me that, having been outspoken on the issues, it would have been deeply hypocritical to cover up my own problems. I just could not do that and look myself in the mirror so, in reality, it was an easy decision. I would take the next six weeks off on sick leave and be public and honest as to why. I would tell the workforce and the community that I needed time to deal with mental and physical exhaustion. On reflection, that was the first day towards wellness.

I summoned my Executive Assistant and my Chief of Staff to my home and disclosed my intentions. They were immediately supportive, if not a little apprehensive as to whether I was taking the right course. Together we concluded that I had taken the right decision. It was now time for action. We devised a communications plan to get the message out. I would advise the government, and email the Victoria Police workforce with a personal message telling them how it was. I would try and lead by example and hoped others would follow. We also informed the community of my hopefully temporary absence in a similar manner. Prior to all of this I would speak with my Command colleagues. I would also request their support and explain the reason for my actions.

It is worth spending a little time at this point detailing the various responses I received. At the outset all were positive. The Police Minister and I agreed on acting arrangements and as to how these would be communicated. She was very understanding and supportive. My Command colleagues to their credit were similarly supportive and immediately agreed to do all they could to fill the breach and be a positive leadership example. My greatest surprise was the positive feedback I received from employees. I was inundated with messages of support from all ranks and locales. Empathy was mixed with thanks for setting the example and practicing what I had been preaching. My ever-vigilant Executive Assistant kept me updated on these responses. With each message I was becoming certain that I had taken the right course and my actions were resonating with the 'unofficial culture' in the organisation. A personal story that could be understood at the station level and, perhaps, provide license for them to speak out and seek support as well. Perhaps more good would come from this than I had anticipated.

Once I had executed this plan, the goal was to rest and recover my health. I had a significant stocktake to do. I had to find balance again in my life – time for work, time for family, time to relax, time to get fitter. I thought back to when I had been most resilient in the past and what behaviours I had in place at that time that led to that state. What were my hobbies? What did I do to relax and clear my head? I also thought about what aspects of my work tired me the most. For me, it was clearly the after-hours events. The representational side of the job was relentless and, if allowed, would occupy every evening of the week. Of course, being Chief Commissioner of Police is a busy role that has many responsibilities. I well understood this and indeed enjoyed the many challenges. The trick though was to find the work/life balance that would enable me to be at optimal health to best meet these challenges.

I developed a new plan dedicated to my own wellness. I would delegate some of my after-hours representational work to my immediate team and where necessary, my broader command team. I am grateful that they eagerly agreed to this. This would recover some of my evenings to spend with the family. Of course, an evening with my family would still include a steady stream of sms messages, crime alerts, and regular phone calls – but at least I would be physically present. I also recommended walking as much as I could, particularly to work. And I reinvested in both vegetable gardening and my long dormant hobby of low and slow American style BBQ. This last endeavour would become a bit of an obsession, with me joining a competition BBQ team with friends and competing in events across the state. My BBQ skills are—I am told— now greatly enhanced, as is my apparent need to share these skills. My generally supportive Chief of Staff would look at his watch and sigh every time someone in the office mentioned BBQ.

After six weeks off, I returned to work. I did so with more energy than before and although the first few weeks were regularly punctuated with people asking me if I was ok, they soon saw that I was confident, that I could work effectively and sustainably with the changes I had made and was making. That period after my return was also a chance to reply to the many messages of support I had received from the workforce. Although my email inbox was usually vetted by office staff due to volume and the regular need for immediate response, I felt it was important to deal with these messages personally. What was clear to me was that my actions had struck a chord. The boss 'leading by example' was a regular theme I was pleased to see. What I also received were many deeply personal experiences that staff felt that they could now share with me. I can only hope that my replies did them justice. Even though I had seen and experienced many harrowing encounters of the mental health harm of my colleagues over the years, I was struck by the gravity of what I read. They were lived examples of what the mental health review had told us. It was clear that I had a moral leadership obligation to my work force. Police mental health had to improve, and I was keen to ensure that the overall bettering of police mental health was a key legacy item of my time as Chief Commissioner.

Feedback that I received was not only from serving members and staff, but also from past serving police. It appeared that I had struck a very particular chord with that cohort. Of course, their experiences were varied. A key theme that became clear, however, was that staff decided to leave Victoria Police because they felt unsupported with their mental health issues. Their departure, they reasoned would help heal them. Conversely, they reported that their departure, meant a brief reprieve before their illness returned, leaving them feeling even more alone, stigmatised and ultimately very angry. There is an old saying in Victoria Police: there is nothing more ex than an ex. Once you leave the job, you leave a team of colleagues that you saw day in and day out. Your contact with most of them ceases. Life immediately becomes much more solitary if not lonely. Thereafter, you feel forever like an outsider. From a moral perspective it was clear that on top of their mental health challenges, a significant gap had emerged between what they regarded as their value set with that of the organisation. In that context even the slightest misstep by the organisation in their dealings with them was to them further evidence of that gap. It was clear to me that another leadership challenge had emerged. What could be done to support our former staff and meet this particular moral obligation?

The Cotton Review had made it clear that we did indeed have a moral obligation to come to the aid of former staff dealing with work associated mental health injury. Up to that point we had addressed many of the report's recommendations, but not that particular one. How we were to do this was made more difficult because of the challenge of funding. Legally, beyond injury management and consequent injury payouts, our responsibility did not extend to past serving members, so how could we justify the expenditure of taxpayer funds from the police budget to support them? The Government had been generous to that point in funding a range of our mental health initiatives. I believed we had to get more creative and collaborative to achieve this particular aim.

I could not have had a better partner to collaborate with on former member mental health than the Police Association of Victoria (TPA). For a long period the TPA had been active in this area, funding a small group of dedicated volunteers to deliver welfare and mental health support to an ever-growing cohort of past serving police. These were people who needed a range of services, from general welfare and support, through to clinical treatment. The 'Retired Peer Support Group', as they were known, were in need of support and without further funding they would cease to exist. Extraordinarily, many of their volunteers had exhausted considerable personal funds. More incredibly, many were still dealing with their own lived experiences as retired police. The TPA Secretary and I met to discuss this issue. We needed a financially sustainable professional agency to support the ongoing welfare and mental health needs of past serving police officers in Victoria to bridge the moral gap that had emerged. The initial goals were to raise start-up funds and to raise awareness.

As Chief Commissioner, I believed that leadership was essential in this area. An agency charged with the care of these past members would resolve the moral dilemma of organisational responsibility required of us and as advocated in the Cotton review. The aim of fund raising was to minimise the expenditure of tax-payer funds. If an agency was going to be a reality it would need leadership and commitment from many people. My role was to lead from the front, to influence and generate the required dedication.

In consultation with the TPA, the concept of a fund and awareness raising walk across Victoria emerged and was considered an attractive option. It could pass many rural police stations and remote communities in the state where, not surprisingly, a great number of former police now resided. It was clear to me that my interest in walking was now to be taken to new levels, but could I really walk what was calculated to be 1000 kilometres from Mallacoota in the far south east corner of the state to Mildura in the far north west corner?

From a leadership perspective I had to complete the walk. In short, I had to lead from the front. I did, however, have the added burden of still performing the role of Chief Commissioner while I completed the walk. Perhaps some middle ground could be found. Thanks to some creative minds at the TPA, the idea of the 'Head to Head' walk emerged. I would walk the (hilly) 500 kilometres from Mallacoota to Wangaratta where I would meet 'head to head' the Secretary of the Police Association who would, at the same time, have walked (the hotter and flatter) 500 kilometres from Mildura to Wangaratta. Nine months of preparation then ensued that involved a dedicated support team from both the Victoria Police and the TPA. Corporate sponsorship and media opportunities had to be sought, logistics planned, en-route events organised. The list of requirements was endless but somehow it was completed. I was heartened by the level of enthusiasm for the project and its cause. The entire Command team at Victoria Police were on board and many were prepared to commit to walking with me on various days during the walk to demonstrate their own leadership.

The walk commenced on 1 October 2018. I felt a sense of relief that the project had started. Leaving Mallacoota, farewelled by a number of locals, I had the words of the late former Chief Commissioner Mick Miller ringing in my ears. I had visited him not long before my departure. Pointing a crooked finger in my direction, the doyen of police commissioners remarked solemnly: 'Just remember, you are the Chief Commissioner. If you start this walk you must, above all else, finish it'. Of course, over the next 23 days of the walk I had many other words ringing in my ears. These were the words of numerous, past serving police officers who walked along side me. Each had a lived experience that they wanted to share. Some of them relayed quite harrowing examples of mental health injury. In most cases they had sadly, felt largely unsupported by Victoria Police. While they did not express their concerns in moral terms, clearly they had suffered both a moral and mental health injury—usually inextricably related. Hearing these examples only strengthened my resolve. Tired legs and blisters were a trivial complaint when compared to the challenges many of these people faced each day. My TPA counterpart told me he was hearing the same thing and that his determination was also fortified. We would finish the walk – come what may.

One of the things you learn about leadership is that you do not actually achieve much if you do not lead good people. You might be the best driver in the world, but you cannot win a Grand Prix driving a Morris Minor. I did complete the 23 days of the walk, but it would have been impossible without the dedicated support of my team. I am sure the TPA side of the walk was the same. The never-ending support that was required each day was achieved seamlessly and according to plan. My mobile office was alongside me so work could continue and I could still lead the organisation. I am so grateful to all for that support. The day I finished the walk was one I will long remember. Shaking hands with the TPA Secretary in Wangaratta was a culmination of almost a year's work by many people.

Together we had collectively raised over $600,000 to start what was to become Police Veterans Support Victoria (PVSV). This was to be an agency solely devoted to the welfare of former police employees. In the early stages of planning for the walk the Secretary of the TPA raised the idea of using the term 'veteran' to describe our past serving police. It carried a positive construction as opposed to 'ex' or 'former'. They had not left. Rather, they had completed their service. They were to be revered and respected for their experience. The idea quickly took hold and was well received. By the end of the walk the word 'veteran' had been embraced within the vernacular and used by all. I hope it will be retained into the future.

While I was engaged with the work associated with police veterans, I also became aware of the impact that their loss of identity had on them. Being a police officer had become part of their identity, and their departure had made them feel that they no longer belonged to something they had loved for many years. I determined that a Victoria Police Veterans' identity card could assist in this regard. This is not a new idea, but I thought we could ensure this card had benefits attached to it that would be of use in relation to welfare, health and lifestyle. The card was launched on 23 October 2019 as a joint venture between Victoria Police and PVSV. It contains a range of corporate benefits. Importantly though, for the 5000 plus veterans who have received it to date, it recognises their status as a Police Veteran. It is evidence of their service and that a moral contract still exists. I understand that other Australian states are looking at this concept in their jurisdictions. I hope that it will one day become national. The police family is, after all, national and global.

As I complete 40 years in policing, I hope that I have successfully discharged my leadership responsibilities in terms of both governance and morality, in regard to police mental health. Victoria Police is now on track in developing an effective mental health injury prevention program that will complement its existing improved injury response services. The word 'safety' has been added to the organisation values as an express moral obligation on the part of the employer. I am aware, however, that the development of mental health for policing has many decades ahead of it. Policing leaders will need to ensure that employee and veteran mental health remains a key organisational priority.

As I write, thousands of serving police are turning up for work each day, discharging their responsibilities to the best of their abilities, smiling and laughing with colleagues and being as helpful as they can to those in need. At the same time that they do this, however, many are asking themselves some quite serious questions. Why can't I get a good night's sleep? Why can't I stop my hand shaking? Why am sweating even though its mid-winter? Why am I so short tempered with my wife and kids? And ominously, what will happen to my police career if I tell someone? This is a current day reality that is caused by untreated mental health injury. The other close companions include substance abuse, marriage and relationship breakdown, loss of employment and its tragic end point, death. What perhaps is less considered is to what extent their moral injury has contributed to their mental health, and what can be done to address that.

The above dilemma creates legal and moral leadership challenges for future police executives. Caring for the wellbeing of the people who work for you is the morally right thing to do. A balance must be struck where police leaders achieve their results regarding community safety through ensuring the safety and care of their own people, and not at the expense of it. I have great optimism that with the high quality of police leaders we have in this country, this future balance will be achieved. Finally, I am hopeful that for those that care to look, I may have provided some examples of how such a balance could be achieved.

PART THREE

7 Understanding the lived experience

Andy Rhodes

'*I*f you want to truly understand something, try to change it', suggested the American-German psychologist Kurt Lewin in the early part of the twentieth century. While Lewin is rightly considered to be the founder of social psychology he would have known very little about neuroscience, neuroplasticity and perhaps even less about groups of humans whose lived experience involves exposure to repeated and continuous traumatic events. Emergency Service Personnel (ESPs) are not exclusive in this regard and are arguably far better equipped to handle a trauma-heavy working life than a young child exposed to domestic violence, abuse and other adverse childhood experiences. ESPs are important players, however, in creating a safe, just and compassionate society, given the type of work they do and the vulnerability of their client groups. If we needed reminders of this then the events of 2020 have yet again provided them for us.

To understand the culture of ESPs properly, we need to embark on a journey full of twists and turns and laced with contradictions. It is not for the faint of heart. It is probably why many change programs focus on transactional improvements, where 'return-on-investment' can be swiftly calculated, as opposed to behavioural change. Organisational and personal identity is too strong to address with top down visions or restructures alone which, in my experience, can widen the gap between the Executive and the frontline. When identity is threatened things usually get very messy. But it does not need to be this way.

I will draw on insights into ESP culture gained from setting up Oscar Kilo, the National Police Well-Being Service (NPWS), which supports over 200,000 police officers and staff in England and Wales.[1] My observations benefit from a growing research base covering many aspects of the ESP experience, ranging from trauma exposure through to fatigue as well as many hundreds of conversations with colleagues over the years.

In ESP cultures a sense of our job being 'who we are' rather than simply 'what we do' can feel like a rubber band continually snapping us back to the status quo. In this article I'll put forward the case for investing in organisational wellbeing as an opportunity for systemic organisational progress rather than simply viewing it as a series of activities or interventions. I'll reference my views and opinions with relevant research and some data because while opinions are interesting they are of limited value when unsupported by facts. Having spent the last decade leading on wellbeing for the police service in England and Wales, I have seen research in this area improve massively and with it our understanding of what makes the incredible humans who keep us safe, at all times and in all places, behave the way they do.

Wellbeing is perhaps a slightly 'lightweight' term for a field of work that asks many uncomfortable questions, such as 'where does bias come from?' and 'how much influence does our work have on our belief systems, values and personal identity?'. Having spent the last decade as a Chief Officer I have observed first-hand the cultural change in relation to mental health in the workplace and can add some useful observations drawn from my exit meetings with several hundred retiring officers. [I see everyone who retires face-to-face and we chat informally about their careers and the future]. I have been doing exit meetings for several years and there are some important recurring themes when we take the time to listen. I also meet all new recruits on their first day and, again, there are some common questions that come up time and time again.

While Identity formation is not my area of expertise, I know enough about it to understand how the powerful influences of early childhood and adolescent experiences shape who we are, how we see the world and how we form relationships. As this process occurs well before we enter the workplace, I will focus on the area with which I am more familiar—the influence of emergency service work on our attitudes, behaviours and identities. I will cover three areas.

Making the transition
How the transition into police work from non-ESP life can rapidly change how we see the world, forming patterns of habitual thinking that normalise the abnormal, while shaping our personal and professional identities.

Kick starting a plan using the G. A. I. N. model
The principles we have successfully applied in my own police force of 6000 people to prevent unchecked initial experiences from developing into problems for the organisation, the individual and our communities. I can prove that they work and that they now form the foundation of the national program.

Wellbeing and change
Finally, I will put forward an argument for investing in wellbeing as a vehicle to help deliver change, while at the same time preparing and protecting the incredible people who keep us safe.

Making the transition to ESP
Virginia Woolf once remarked that 'you have your identity when you find out, not what you can keep your mind on, but what you can't keep your mind off'. One of the great parts of my job is meeting new recruits and their families when we 'swear them in' at an attestation ceremony. I am always much encouraged by the constant influx of new recruits to the service. Yet, at the same time, I have a slightly heavy heart because I know what happens next. In a recent analysis of applicants to British policing they reported being interested in joining the police in four key areas: helping young people; supporting victims; and improving communities, with the fourth motivator described as 'thrill-seeking'.

Only 25 per cent rated 'thrill-seeking' as their main motivational factor? Now that would definitely not have been the case amongst my 'band of brothers' (we were mainly men) in the early 1990s. Society has changed and with it the intentions of our new recruits. Given that around 50 per cent of our current establishment have over 18 years of service these tensions play out on a daily basis. In our recent national workforce survey the group reporting feelings of being held back due to their ethnicity and gender were, of course, white males. Ignore such insights at your peril is my advice.

Emergency service work involves high levels of stress. Research has understandably focused on operational exposure to traumatic events as the main cause. It is also recognised that organisational stressors can have a corrosive impact on ESPs mental health.[2] Lack of resources, public criticism, being investigated and unnecessary bureaucracy are examples of organisational stressors common in the emergency services and must be taken into account when considering the new entrant. Policing is an inherently 'risky business' not least because of the high levels of accountability and public scrutiny faced by the service. Risk aversion is high and entails huge levels of non-value work as well as a blame culture, often leaving those nearest to the work feeling poorly supported and undervalued.

When we examine research into moral injury this is where it probably starts. Optimistic, purposeful and positive humans who have probably never seen a dead body or been in a fight walk through our doors and enter a world where they very quickly realise it is not quite as straightforward as they had imagined. Ours is the world of the so-called 'wicked problem' where making a difference can very quickly feel out of reach only to be replaced with a sense of hopelessness manifesting in a detached sense of 'going through the motions'.

ESPs spend the vast proportion of their day with a small but very intense client group. The levels of intergenerational vulnerability, mental health, exploitation and violence come as an immediate shock to the system and, of course, to the ESP brain which is soon scrambling to make sense of what it is now seeing and experiencing day in day out. Help is, however, at hand. The research tells us quite a lot about what faces your new 'asset'. It is a considerably long list given policing involves 'high emotional labour'.

To begin with a few major headlines:

Around 1 in 5 may have undiagnosed PTSD or Complex PTSD.

93 per cent of the 1 in 5 with undiagnosed PTSD or CPTSD have not reported sick.[3]

Around 65 per cent will have severe sleep deprivation getting less than 6 hours sleep a night.

70 per cent feel undervalued by their organisation and the public.

92 per cent of people report high levels of pride in their work.[4]

Plainly, many people are traumatized and exhausted but remain incredibly proud of the contribution they make to society.

The fact that most of these 'assets' are behaving impeccably well at 3am is more a testament to their character than any deliberate organisational action. When they don't live up to the high standards expected (which one could argue are unrealistic to start with) their lived experience is rarely, if ever, considered. Note, I use the work 'considered' as I do not suggest we use the research as an excuse for bad behaviour or poor standards. Research is, however, vital contextual information. Let me return to where it starts.

We are not zebras

New ESP experiences build on the brain's well-established negativity-bias which, of course, is an excellent defence mechanism helping us to 'fight or flight' in milliseconds. In *Why Zebras Don't Get Ulcers*, Robert Sapolsky compares the human response to a threat with those of the zebra. The zebra's brain responds to a threat in much the same way as the human brain but as soon as the immediate threat is gone the zebra does not ruminate or worry about how the experience felt or the desperateness of the situation. It simply returns to munching grass. Humans respond differently to zebras and Sapolsky suggests this is why stress can overwhelm us, changing the way we think and feel, sometimes with consequences such as mental illness and/or associated physical illnesses such as ulcers.

Rick Hanson combines his passion for Buddhism with neuroscience and explains how we can re-wire our brains.

> Changing your mind for the better means changing your brain for the better. The brain is continually re-modelling itself as you learn from your experiences. When you repeatedly stimulate a 'circuit' in your brain you strengthen it. You learn to be calmer, more compassionate the way you learn anything else—through repeated practice.[5]

Jeff Thompson, of the New York Police Department, sets out the vital ingredients of ESP resilience training in another chapter in this volume. He reveals the antithesis of the mindset we reward and instill into our ESPs. That is his point - our brains already have an inbuilt negativity bias and will default to pessimistic thinking because that is how we survive. Therefore, before we even enter the intense world of the ESP our brains have an inbuilt tendency towards pessimistic thinking.

ESPs are required to think the worst. We reward this thinking and it has some very positive outcomes when it comes to catching bad people. Repeated enough times any thought pattern will become habitual. As Rick Hanson says 'neurons that fire together wire together'. Habitual thinking can change our belief systems and along with this change our identity. Hyper-vigilance is the hallmark of the great street cop ... the thief taker we all admire, is it not? I find it very hard to relax when off duty because I suffer from hyper-vigilance and, without exception, I hear this from retirees with different levels of severity. An operational necessity, a key ESP strength we know very little about.

In his 2008 book *Outliers*, Malcolm Gladwell suggests that when we repeat an act for 10,000 hours we develop 'instinct and intuition'. Perhaps for an ESP we might recognise an unfathomable feeling that 'something just ain't right here'. On a rough calculation of 250 working days per annum on an 8-hour shift (very rare for ESPs), that is 2080 hours a year. Thus in 5 years an ESP's gut instinct is formed which is, of course, generally a good thing. Or is it? Perhaps only until our gut instinct starts to form pejorative opinions of people and places. Until gut instinct leads to bias (unconscious or otherwise) about certain types of people, how they look, walk or speak. With no brakes applied this incredible ESP strength, like all strengths overplayed, risks becoming our greatest weakness.

So how does this help us explain ESP culture? For me, Martin Seligman, the founder of positive psychology, hits the nail firmly on the head when he describes the type of thinking which can develop into a habitual mindset left unchecked. I defy anyone who has worked as an ESP (or among ESPs) to say they do not recognise some aspects of what I am about to describe in either themselves or others.

The four Ps

Martin Seligman describes four ways—the Ps—in which we tend to deal with hard things in life when they happen repeatedly. First, personalisation: thinking you are the problem. Second, permanence: thinking a bad situation will last forever or perpetuate. Third, pervasiveness: thinking a bad situation applies to every aspect of your life or society. Fourth, pejorative: judgemental, derogatory thinking often disparaging and critical. This is how I thought in the mid-1990s.

> Everyone who lives in this part of town hates the police because they are all criminals and, therefore, they also hate me. Their parents were the same and in time their kids will be the same. It's always been this way and always will be ... there's nothing anyone can do to break the cycle. I joined this job to make a difference and improve things but the world is an awful place so there's no hope left.

Does this sound familiar? In my experience it is at this point where researchers and academics exit stage left and the people who are supposed to be in charge are asked to do something about it. Describing the problem is important but it is never enough. The leadership team may want to do something but be unsure where to start or they may simply shrug their shoulders adopt the 4 Ps and say: 'it has always been this way'. This is code for 'they are not going to do anything about it'. After spending the last eight years immersed in the research and making all the mistakes there are to make, I can offer some advice before embarking on your wellbeing journey. You need a plan informed by research as well as a deep analysis of how your people are feeling, thinking and behaving. You simply cannot ignore it.

Kick staring a plan using the G. A. I.N model
Dr Ian Hesketh and Sir Cary Cooper published a paper to which I contributed in 2016. It was titled 'Measuring the people fleet—General Analysis of Interventions & Need' or G. A. I. N. [6] Our purpose was to help facilitate planning sessions with various leadership groups interested in wellbeing and who did not know where to start. By applying GAIN we can begin to assess who is doing 'ok', who is 'struggling to cope', who is 'not coping' and who is in 'crisis', helping them work out that investing in prevention is far better than in cure. Another reason was to map engagement against assessment of need, to identify missed opportunities. Misconduct, poor performance, falling victim, satisfaction rates and high overtime would often correlate directly with escalating mental health need. By presenting the analysis process as a familiar early intervention model we help ESP teams apply the same principles to themselves and to those they lead.

General Analysis, Interventions and Needs (GAIN) Pyramid

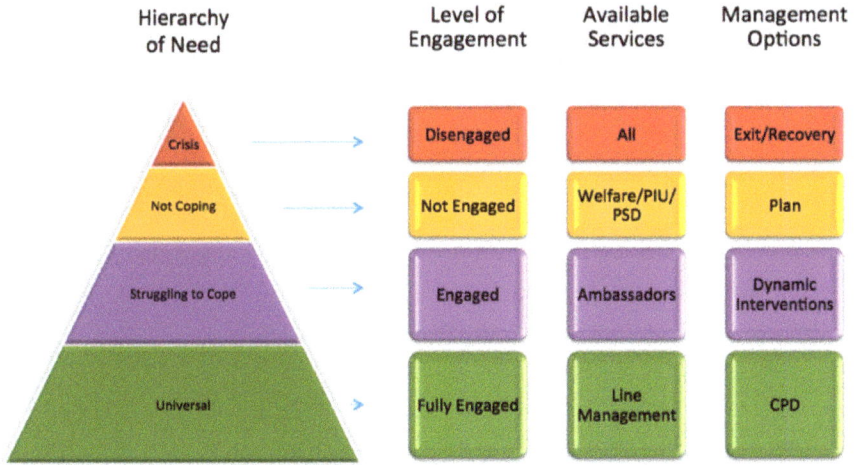

Hierarchy of Need	Level of Engagement	Available Services	Management Options
Crisis	Disengaged	All	Exit/Recovery
Not Coping	Not Engaged	Welfare/PIU/PSD	Plan
Struggling to Cope	Engaged	Ambassadors	Dynamic Interventions
Universal	Fully Engaged	Line Management	CPD

© IHAR2015

Using available 'people' data we can start to populate the model to understand the health of the workforce, ranging from 'doing ok' to 'crisis' As a diagnostic tool the GAIN model will usually identify the following issues:

Your 'people' data is inadequate because it only measures what is easily available as opposed to what is relevant to achieving the organisational purpose.

70% + will be categorised as 'doing ok' but as Cooper observed 'the absence of illness does not mean we are well'. Recent research by Jess Miller from Cambridge University suggests as many as one in five police officers have undiagnosed PTSD.

The actual number of people 'in crisis' will be very low yet they will be attracting a significant amount of organisational time, effort and conversation. Most of them will be waiting to be released, pending misconduct or in non-operational roles that are not budgeted.

As we talk through the model it becomes apparent that, on any given day, a frontline ESP will ebb and flow between 'doing ok' to 'crisis'. The question will be one of resilience. Do they easily return to doing ok or escalate slowly to 'struggling to cope' and 'not coping' without noticing?

When we challenge traditional notions of 'coping' we start to see resilience in a different light, as negative versions of resilience such as alcohol consumption and 'game face' are discussed.

Alongside the model we see management options, levels of engagement and available services. It becomes clear that, as a person's failure to cope escalates, they become disengaged, the management options become more intense and the services required become more specialist and expensive.

Leadership teams start to question the status quo as they relate their own experiences to the model, noting lost opportunities aplenty.

Attending to these issues means we start seeing where the opportunities exist to improve what many leaders believe to be a permanent, impenetrable aspect of ESP life. Leaders also need hope.

We see the case for investing in the areas that make the most difference which are also the highest 'Return-on-Investment' given many are cost neutral.

There is no cost to a line manager taking a few minutes out to sit quietly with a member of staff who they have spotted behaving out of character and simply asking 'are you ok?' followed by 'but are you *really* ok?'.

There is no cost to creating a team culture where people feel comfortable disclosing how they are feeling after a difficult job or because they are preoccupied worrying about the health of a loved one.

There is very little cost in recognising the value of social networks other than to see them as a force for good rather than a threat to data security.

There is no cost incurred when we have an honest conversation with someone who is not taking personal responsibility for their own physical or mental health when support is available.

One significant aspect of ESP culture is the level of discretionary effort that they will give above and beyond their standard remuneration. It may come in the guise of staying connected to a victim's family long after the conviction is sealed or in the willingness of ESPs to repeatedly put themselves in harm's way. Yet, we cannot, and should never, take discretionary effort for granted because it can be withdrawn as we can see using the GAIN model. If discretionary effort is the lifeblood of ESP work then a well thought through approach to wellbeing is the fuel that keeps it alive by shifting the mindset of the whole organisation towards one that is strengths-based, building high trust and positive resilience.

Key planning principles

Principle 1   **You don't know what it feels like anymore**

To grab the Executive team's attention, I usually start with a provocative slide entitled 'The Iceberg of Ignorance' because most ESP leaders believe they know more than they do about the lived experience of the people on their frontline. We rarely do. Research tells us that Executives see about 3 per cent, C-Suites see around 11 per cent, line managers 36 per cent and, of course, those nearest the work see 100 per cent. This is a 97 per cent reality gap. Get over it before you start the wellbeing plan.

A great wellbeing plan does not have a start and an end. It is an iterative, learning process which must sit complementary to the change and business planning disciplines. Kurt Lewin understood that real, lasting change only happens through dialogue. Yet, for most executives the open, authentic dialogue can feel like an uphill struggle particularly in hierarchical cultures where rank and authority create filters between those 'in the work' and the boardroom.

Before kick starting a plan suppress the ego and practice humility. Open up multiple channels of feedback to increase employee voice and genuine engagement. I have found staff engagement to be a real challenge for many leadership teams, having invested significant time, money and attention on this activity over the last eight years. It is humbling, the source of much criticism and rarely the focus of any thanks. But when done well it is the single most influential factor in any wellbeing plan because it creates a foundation of legitimacy and connection with the workforce from the outset.

Organisations are complex systems driven by social networks of humans, networks you have little control over and have to be invited into. Unless you recognise the power of networks and, therefore, accept the limitations of hierarchical command structures you will never build the trust needed to improve wellbeing. The good news is wellbeing, mental health, trauma and fatigue are fertile grounds to engage with ESPs. Dr Ian Hesketh and I facilitated an @WeCops Twitter debate on police workforce mental health that reached over 3.8 million people. You need to talk about what your people are interested in and they are far more interested in wellbeing than your corporate vision and 5-year Medium Term Financial Strategy. Get them talking and you will reap the rewards.

Principle 2   I believe what I see

As previously discussed we ESPs can be a suspicious crowd, especially when we hear about 'strategies' and 'visions' heading our way from on high. When you invest in Principle 1, you will see that most people come to work to do the best job they can. Their wellbeing is affected by the basics of any well-run organisation: sufficient resources to meet demand; competent and fair line managers; high autonomy; low bureaucracy; adequate training and equipment. Logistics matter a lot.

Every organisation wants to get this right because it drives the bottom line. Whether it is talent attraction, staff turnover, customer satisfaction or quality the basics need to be as good as they can be and so it is for the ESPs. The only difference is the nature of the work which amplifies their emotional response to any change away from the status quo. The ESP cup is already pretty full so invest in getting the basics right to improve their wellbeing. Wellbeing must never be used to mitigate the harmful effects of a poorly run organisation. Similarly, resilience training must never be used to develop coping strategies to protect individuals from the avoidable stresses of organisational life. Some days just fixing the printer might be enough.

Principle 3   People before process

Several years ago the Police Superintendents Association of England and Wales surveyed its 1150 members to determine the foremost source of stress. Myths were shattered as respondents rarely cited command of firearms, public order or serious crime investigation as being the main causes of stress. Instead 'dealing with complex HR issues' topped the list. That's because most organisations still use coercive absence management policies which escalate 'meetings' through the command chain. By the time a superintendent has a 'meeting', the case is so complex it is usually too late to recover.

The 43 police forces in England and Wales use the evidence-based Oscar Kilo Blue light Assessment Framework to benchmark their progress and rate themselves accordingly. Our analysis conducted by the University of Central Lancashire's Professor Stuart Kirby identified absence management as the 'most developed' area. On a separate piece of research, carried out through structured interviews with over 300 staff, we sought to identify which organisational policies created the most stress. Top of the list was, rather predictably, the absence management policy.

Forces were rating themselves as 'well developed' in absence management because it is what they were spending huge amounts of time, money and leadership effort on, not because it was actually working. This was a moment of illumination. It is making people even more ill. It is a common story. The great cop who suddenly loses their way and, for no apparent reason, starts to fall foul of the organisational checks and balances, often resulting in the wrong solution being applied to the right problem. Just like we are urged to think differently when we meet a prolific offender with complex needs (usually originating from early childhood trauma), we must pause and ask fewer questions about what is happening today and more questions about how the person got here. What went before is the story, the context and where deeper understanding will emerge to help us intervene earlier.

Wellbeing and change

It has taken me a long time, through trial and error, to know where to start and that is because I failed to start with the correct 'why' question. Of course, wellbeing is a good thing for us but it is important to recognise that not everything which affects our wellbeing, morale, motivation, mental health and happiness is work-related. In fact, when we analyse our surveys we see 'life' outside of work as having far more relevance. The first step, therefore, is to avoid either assuming responsibility for everything or avoiding the subject because it is not all within your grasp.

When the United Kingdom's Office of National Statistics (ONS) published its workforce attitudes survey, I was drawn to using the findings to answer the 'why' question. Their interviews and surveys with tens of thousands of people show us that, in terms of overall life satisfaction, we peak around age 18 and then descend into a bell curve of ever lowering satisfaction until we bottom out around age 54. As I am approaching my 55th birthday, I am looking forward to slowly inching my way back to my 18 year old self although, according to the ONS, I will be around 72 by the time the level of early adulthood returns! This sounds counter-intuitive and unreal. Do we really peak at 18?

So the 'why' question is this. As an organisational leader who is privileged to hold the lives of ESPs in your hands while they are working for you, is your workplace going to make their already challenging lives better or worse? Every piece of research or workforce survey highlights the fact that it is rarely the nature of the work alone which makes us psychologically and, therefore, physically unwell. Rather, it is the trials and tribulations of organisational life that are the principal origins.[7] Bureaucracy, leadership behaviour, poor technology, internal processes and policies that treat people as if they are all the same are factors. I could go on.

The nature of the work requires an investment in the right specialist support but this alone is not enough. If the ESP's capacity is nearing exhaustion, one more additional burden can render them incapable of continuing. When change is being introduced and someone reacts in a seemingly disproportionate way, suspend judgement and consider the reason. Their reaction may not be about the change itself but the 'drip, drip' effect of countless other events that have led them to feeling devalued or criticised. It is not unlike an argument with a partner. The matter at issue may be the cause but it is rarely the source. The argument is about the multitude of unspoken slights and undisclosed shortcomings that have gone before.

Leaders must start by accepting our limitations and recognising our work will never end. Our job is to create a psychologically and physically safe space for the ESPs for whom we have accepted responsibility. When seen as the 'why', other metrics will usually fall into line. Reduced absenteeism, decreased misconduct, improved talent attraction and lower staff turnover are equally applicable in any employment sector. In my experience, the lifeblood of any ESP organisation is practicing compassion and managing risk. Often when working with executive teams I see eyes glaze over ahead of being asked the usual hard question: 'prove' well-being is a worthwhile investment. I will always appeal to their hearts by raising compassion as the hallmark of any victim experience. But remaining compassionate is extremely challenging for ESPs. If this line of reasoning fails, I focus on the operational business case and talk about risk with a few scenarios.

For instance, research shows that your most public-facing asset has been taking annual leave instead of calling in sick and has had several rest days cancelled due to unforeseen operational demand. Most of these people are getting less than 6 hours sleep a night and 20 per cent are suffering from some form of undetected or undiagnosed post-traumatic stress. Only a third feel valued by the organisation and the public. Add to this mindset regular exposure to social media footage of fellow officers being assaulted and relentless criticism from mainstream media. These are ordinary humans doing an extraordinary job, entrusted with far reaching power and authority by the state. Many, if not all, are driving cars very fast and carrying firearms or other less lethal weapons. Every decision, action and word are judged against a necessarily high standard. My question to the executive team, having gained their attention, is this: 'are you satisfied you have a well thought through plan in place to mitigate the risk I have just described?'. Do you even understand how they are *thinking* and *feeling*?

Competing personal and organisational responsibility

At this point I usually introduce the most important element of wellbeing and resilience: personal responsibility. If a person chooses to embark upon a career as an ESP there is a legitimate expectation from their employer that they will take personal responsibility for their physical and psychological health and ensure it remains good. Many overlook this responsibility. Echoing the remarks in Jeff Thompson's chapter on resilience, the critical component of personal resilience is self-awareness. Numerous colleagues say they 'never seeing it coming', revealing they were unaware at an emotional and psychological level that they were entering a mental health crisis until it was too late.

Surveys from the main police unions and staff associations track significant improvements in key areas relating to workforce mental health particularly stigma reduction. Thanks to many role models and the support of numerous charities, over 80 per cent of staff surveyed now say they feel confident talking openly about their mental health. This represents a 30 per cent increase in two years. But now they are talking, are we listening? Even more importantly, are we responding with a good plan and the requisite resources—financial and human? It takes commitment from both employer and employee in equal amounts.

Final thoughts

Seligman advocates 'practical optimism'. It is a brand of positive thinking grounded in the often harsh realities of life, making it highly suitable for most ESPs. While I have painted a deliberately honest picture of the ESP experience, and could be forgiven for negativity bias, leaders must strive at all times to be optimistic and re-frame the purpose of ESP work rather than shy away from its trials and tribulations. When I speak with new recruits and retiring officers, our conversations move towards framing our work as a privilege, a purposeful endeavour full of meaning and pride. To be with someone in an hour of need will often require the leader to become second victim, spending precious moments by their side and experiencing their trauma. For victims of crime or misadventure, the experience may be a singular one. The ESP must strive to make it bearable, playing an important part in their eventual recovery. Contrastingly, for the ESP this experience will be repeated hundreds of times throughout their careers. To be 'present' and 'compassionate' will have a toll on their mental and physical health, as well as their personal and private lives. No wonder then that identities are formed early and seem to endure long after public service has ended.

The leader's role is to commit time, attention and resources to help them do what society asks of them. Wellbeing can be a non-judgmental focal point to support ESPs. It must be placed at the forefront of 'how we do change' rather than as an afterthought or a bolt-on specialist function. Wellbeing is, in its purest sense, a vehicle for generating meaningful dialogue about how the nature of work affects our mental and physical health. But it is far more than this. Wellbeing is also a vehicle for understanding how informal systems or networks operate within the organisational culture and it is also a vehicle for developing empathy, compassion and trust. These are the true benchmarks of excellence for Emergency Service Personnel.

Endnotes

1   www.oscarkilo.org.uk

2   R Nicholas Carleton; *International Journal of Environmental Research and Public Health*, 2020.

3   CB Brewin, JK Miller, M Soffia and B Burchell, 'Posttraumatic Stress Disorder and Complex Posttraumatic Stress Disorder in UK Police Officers', *Journal of Clinical Psychology*, 2020 forthcoming.

4   *National Well Being Survey England & Wales*, number 35,000, 2020.

5   Rick Hanson, *Resilience: find your inner strength*, 2018.

6   This paper suggests that the use of an appropriate strategic HR model, such as the General Analysis, Interventions and Needs (GAIN) pyramid (Hesketh and Rhodes, 2015), can assist organisations to develop practical categories and metrics to illustrate employee status in relation to wellbeing. The arguments posed provide opportunities for practitioners to use workforce-modelling tools that assist in identifying, categorising and targeting wellbeing interventions in the workplace. This paper highlights that identifying, categorising and prioritising wellbeing interventions in the workplace has hitherto received little academic attention. This paper contributes by providing a greater practical insight into what may work, which is important for leaders in all organisations, particularly those trying to maintain operational performance while undergoing programmes of change. Ian Hesketh and Cary Cooper, 'Measuring the people fleet: general analysis, interventions and needs', *Strategic HR Review*, vol. 16 No. 1, 2017, pp. 17–23.

7   See figure 1 below. Source: C Naylor, et. al., (2012) Report. "Long term conditions and mental health. The cost of co-morbidities, The King's Fund and Centre for Mental Health.

Figure 1 The overlap between long-term conditions and mental health problems

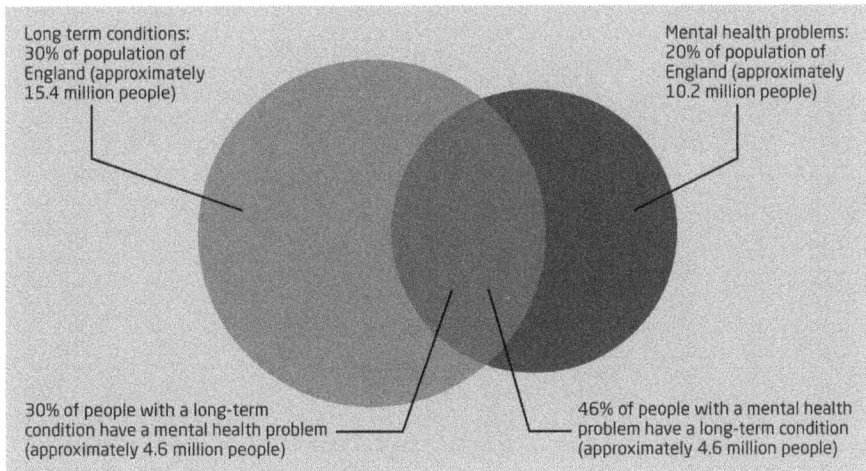

Long term conditions: 30% of population of England (approximately 15.4 million people)

Mental health problems: 20% of population of England (approximately 10.2 million people)

30% of people with a long-term condition have a mental health problem (approximately 4.6 million people)

46% of people with a mental health problem have a long-term condition (approximately 4.6 million people)

8 First responders and real resilience

Jeff Thompson

*F*irst responders are often described as 'superheroes' for the work that they do. With that perception comes a constant but invisible burden for the individual responder. Outwardly, people see larger-than-life men and women rushing towards danger, saving others in distress, solving complex and horrific crimes, and keeping their cool amid chaos. The ability to remain calm and collected and to display professionalism rightfully garners the respect and admiration of those whom first responders serve. It is worth considering, however, the toll that playing the role of a real-life superhero may take.

It is common knowledge that first responders, and especially those involved in law enforcement, have high rates of insomnia, depression, anxiety, post-traumatic stress disorder (PTSD) and suicide. In part, this is because they experience traumatic events at much higher rates than members of the general public. According to one estimate, law enforcement officers may witness as many as two hundred such events during their careers.

Members of the public might well ask why these superheroes are so susceptible to such mental health conditions. An obvious source of stress for them is the weight of expectations on the part of the public, media, politicians, and even co-workers and the officers themselves. The fact is that first responders exacerbate the excessive demands that are placed on them by failing to take the kind of care of, and show the kind of compassion towards, themselves that they show to those whom they protect and serve on a daily basis. Their various mental health conditions are the result, and they can, in extreme cases, lead to premature death. Perhaps saddest of all are the lives cut short when some of these professionals, after having saved countless strangers, take their own lives.

The officers themselves do not deserve the blame for the ailments that they suffer as a result of their employment. It is both pointless and unfair to ask, in such situations, 'Why didn't she reach out for help?' or 'Why didn't he take care of himself?' or 'Why did this happen when so many free services were available to her?' Efforts to encourage members of law enforcement to seek help through awareness and outreach campaigns and the provision of mental health services have brought about some real advances in the profession. Necessary conversations are happening much more frequently than was the case just a few years ago, and the leaders of many agencies have made mental health a priority. As a result, first responders are becoming more open to the concept of checking in with and encouraging each other to seek help when they need it. All too frequently, however, those who urge others to take care of themselves are not necessarily practicing what they preach.

This unfortunate situation is a kind of inversion of the famous aphorism in the 1989 movie *Field of Dreams* that, 'If you build it, they will come'. There have been remarkable advances in the services available to members of law enforcement, but they are not used near as often as they should be given the high incidence of mental health conditions in the first responder profession. We built it, but they did not come. There is no ready explanation as to why this mental health infrastructure is not helping more officers who need it. The discussion here concerns how first responders can map out a path forward through their own stress, anxiety, tension, trauma, and struggles and those of the people whom they help every day, a path for individuals and the profession as a whole toward positive mental health habits and resilience. This path leads to a smoother career trajectory as members of law enforcement embrace the support that is available when things become difficult, intense, and even overwhelming (which they certainly will) and persevere in positive ways.

In this chapter, I share my experiences assisting my brothers and sisters in blue in numerous agencies and various countries. My role has ranged from helping a fellow officer to access immediate, professional help to interacting with others while they recovered and navigated their current issues to having a cup of coffee with those who need a sympathetic and non-judgemental ear. I have had the privilege of travelling the world and being able to witness in person what true strength looks like. The following are some of the stories of the first responders I have met.[1] These are stories of despair, tragedy, pain, suffering, and anguish experienced by remarkable human beings who, ultimately, turned them into stories of recovery, hope, and triumph.

'With my left hand, I picked up the phone'

Sarah was going through a lot. She was a single mother of a daughter not yet in school. Her mother helped out as much as possible, and work was accommodating—at least at first. Her initial supervisor was the kind of boss for whom you would do anything, the kind you would think about years later and say 'I wish all bosses were like that'. He adjusted Sarah's schedule when necessary and was always checking in on her to see how she was doing. This supervisor helped her to manage things, but in truth she was struggling. She had felt depressed ever since the birth of her daughter; she described it as always feeling like she was 'in a funk'. All day, she felt dull and lethargic and lacked motivation; it took all of her energy to complete even simple tasks. She 'only just was getting by', then, her best-ever supervisor was promoted and moved on.

Her new supervisor was the exact opposite of the previous one, the kind his employees would remember years later as 'the boss worst ever'. He would not accommodate her with any schedule changes and told her to toughen up and leave her personal issues at home because 'the police department is not a daycare facility'. Once she even overheard him describing her to other officers as a 'scammer' always looking to get time off from work and as too 'soft'. Sarah used to look forward to going to work as an escape from the pressures of her personal life, but now work was a second hell. Exacerbating her plight, she was not sleeping. She told me that she felt as if she were in a dark hole with dirt falling on her. She was stuck, and it was only getting worse.

One evening, while sitting on her couch, she had her firearm in her hand. The television was turned off; she was just sitting there. Looking back, she recalled, the lack of sleep had driven her to the edge; she felt that she could no longer handle the pressure. She told me that she had never thought that she would have suicidal thoughts, not in a million years, but now, with the added sleep deprivation, she found herself feeling hopeless and helpless; she was isolated and did not see how things could ever get better. She just did not want to live anymore more.

At that moment, she made a choice. With her agency-issued firearm still in her right hand, she shared, 'with my left hand, I picked up the phone'. She decided that she could not go on alone anymore and made a phone call to get the help that she needed and deserved. Now, a few years later, Sarah is full-duty, working patrol, and protecting her great city as she had always wanted to do. You would never know her story of overcoming adversity by looking at her. She could be that young officer working on the day shift with you right now. Think about that for a few moments.

'It was the best fish and chips I ever had'

For a while, Henry had everything. He was a high-ranking supervisor in his agency, handsome, fit, and friendly while also always professional. In short, he had his act together. Then, he 'ruined everything'. He cheated on his wife with a co-worker. As he explained it, there was a gathering after his shift at a local pub where he 'had a few more than a few' beers. That was the norm; the motto for him and many of his mates had been 'work hard, play hard'. There was a woman there with whom he had often flirted and who seemed to flirt back. One thing led to another and, he told me, fueled by alcohol, he had made a bad decision. His wife found out and left with the kids and the dog. Neither her family nor his wanted to talk to him. His life spiraled out of control. After more than 20 years of service spent looking ahead to what he thought would be a life with his family in retirement, he was now staring into the unknown.

I did not know Henry at the time, since he worked in another agency, but, as the saying goes, a 'friend of a friend' reached out to me and asked whether I would be willing to talk with him. So, we talked. Among the reasons that I am sharing this story here is to show the kind of help that is effective when someone is going through a hard time and experiencing mental anguish. I have received great training from amazing trainers on the 'dos and don'ts' in these circumstances.

I knew that I was not going to solve or 'fix' Henry's problems; such a mindset would be unrealistic and ineffective when someone is going through a personal crisis. A common feeling among people going through personal crises like this is that they have no control over their lives, and it might seem that you have all the right answers. The key question in this case, though, is whether a point-by-point game plan laying out what the person in crisis needs to do is actually going to be helpful, that is, whether such a plan would empower someone who feels powerless.

This is where the art of listening—better, active listening—comes into play. Active listening skills are the go-to techniques for hostage negotiators (I have worked as a negotiator and trainer) and crisis counselors at great organisations like Crisis Text Line (where I am a volunteer counselor). This kind of listening involves emotional labeling, paraphrasing, asking open-ended questions, and, above all, giving individuals in crisis the opportunity to talk and know that they have been both heard and understood. These active listening skills are the 'science' of crisis communication, while the 'art' is using them effectively to build genuine rapport, develop trust, and manage tension and negative emotions. Using these skills to help someone in a personal crisis is also about validating and normalising what individuals in crisis are feeling. These feelings need to be acknowledged rather than ignored, minimised, or drowned out with 'happy thoughts'.

By slowing things down and not rushing toward a resolution, individuals like Henry are able to think more clearly, to feel calmer, to act more rationally, and to be open to ideas and suggestions from people who care about their welfare. The realisation that emotions and feelings directly impact an individual's actions helps him or her to figure out the best path forward. Then, the approach of trying to move forward in a positive manner becomes a team effort rather than an attempt to identify a quick fix that ends with the person trying to help saying, 'Here's what you need to do.'

Henry was feeling depressed about the turmoil in his life and worried about what to do next (such as whether to reconcile with his wife). As a consequence, he was experiencing insomnia symptoms, lack of appetite, and constant headaches; like Sarah, he felt as if he were in a 'mind fog'. He was not sure whether his drinking was an issue. The only positive thing that he could still see in his life was that he continued to work out in the gym. When he mentioned this, I immediately said, 'It is great that you're working out; but what about your mental workouts?'

In order to help Henry, I listened while he told his story and made clear to him that his feelings were normal for someone in his situation. It sounds simple, but this form of communication can have a powerful positive impact on people in crisis, serving as a reality check for law enforcement officers.

We need to remind ourselves and each other that we are not robots devoid of feeling and also that there are proven methods for ensuring that negative emotions do not overwhelm us and dictate our actions. I also reminded Henry that he was not alone and encouraged him to be fair to himself. A good way to better his situation, I told him, was by looking after himself. He replied that he did not know how or where to start, and I said that we would take on one issue at a time and be careful not to add to the anxiety that he was already experiencing. As the saying goes, the best way to eat an elephant is one bite at a time.

Therefore, we talked first about sleep, and Henry agreed that seeking professional help in this regard made sense since he could possibly be prescribed medication as well as receive guidance from a mental health professional. Dealing with his sleep issues would set him on the path to recovery with a clearer and calmer mind with which to figure out how to confront his other issues. Again, this approach was critical for helping him to establish a perspective from which to work out how best to navigate his current situation.

As our conversation concluded, I told Henry, 'I want you to do something for me'. Then I asked him to have a meal that evening that he would truly enjoy because he deserved a pleasurable experience amid all that he was going through and everything he was feeling. I told him to do this, not as a way to downplay the seriousness of his situation, but as a step toward ending his downward spiral. If we make room for the 'bad', I said, it is only fair that we also make some room for the 'good' too. This is self-compassion, and it is a key component of hard-core resilience.

If Henry was going to halt his downward spiral, it would need to be through his own doing. His path to recovery started with small-scale actions that reminded him that he was in control of his own life and capable of looking after himself. As we parted, I asked him to text me that evening to let me know what he had had for his meal. The rest of my day went by rapidly, and, before I knew it, I was back home on the couch watching television. My phone dinged at 2127 hours; it was a text from Henry. 'I got myself that meal. It was the best fish and chips I ever had.'

In my work on resiliency, peer support, and crisis counseling, I frequently tell people that, when measuring success, first consider the scale that you are using. Henry's personal crisis was not going to be resolved as a result of our one conversation, but that conversation could still have a profound impact in terms of improving his situation. Taking things one day at a time, one moment at a time, is not a cliché. It is realistic, and it works for individuals navigating a personal crisis. Self-compassion of this sort involves acknowledging that we all experience setbacks and hardships and not kicking ourselves when we are already down. It means treating ourselves the same way that we would treat a close friend or loved one going through a similar experience.

'Go figure, breathing works'

Anthony, a police officer, had been experiencing anxiety. When I asked him for how long, he answered 'forever'. When I asked what was currently causing him stress, he answered, 'everything'. As we talked, he opened up more and shared with me that his teenage son, a star soccer player, was seeking a college scholarship but had been switched to another team because he was not getting along with his teammates. Amid multiple offers from various schools, the family was worried about choosing the wrong one as well as the situation on his current team and his ability to maintain his grades so as to be eligible for scholarships. At work, Anthony said, he had been thinking about these issues constantly.

All of this was occurring during the COVID-19 pandemic, and Anthony was concerned about bringing the virus home. A family summer camping vacation had to be cancelled, and he felt that he and his family were being cheated. With the emergence of anti-police protests, he said that he felt constantly angry at the public for labelling all police as racists and became enraged at media coverage of policing and what he described as the stupidity of social media. He spoke of watching over his infant daughter while she slept to make sure that she was still breathing. He said that he had given up drinking because that only frayed his nerves further.

I asked him what he was doing to help himself get through each day. 'Nothing, nothing at all', he replied. He said that his mind seemed like a jukebox stuck on repeat but, instead of a song, it was replaying his worries. His symptoms were not only psychological, he explained, 'It's made me sick. Physically sick, I'd throw up'.

Depression has been described as worrying about the past and anxiety as worrying about the future. In either case, the sufferer is not living in the present moment. Many individuals suffer from both depression and anxiety simultaneously, which is said to be like having a devil perched on each shoulder. It is hard to know what to say to people in this condition; just thinking about it can cause anxiety in those who seek to help them. This is the phenomenon of empathic distress, which arises when caregivers forget to look after themselves amid their constant efforts to help others. The result can be compassion fatigue and burnout.

Sometimes, the language that is used is a key consideration in efforts to help others, which is another way of saying that the messenger can be as important as the message. When I was interacting with Anthony, I chose my words and approach in part based on the fact that he was a tough, macho sort (not in a bad way) working in a SWAT-type unit. I knew that, for now at least, it would be counterproductive to discuss self-compassion, mindfulness, and meditation with him using those terms. Therefore, I needed to figure out a way to encourage him to look after himself and by embracing these strategies but using terms that would be meaningful to him and not cause him to dismiss what I was saying out of hand.

The task was daunting, but I was not going to abandon him. Instead, I used other terms and referred to practices that had proved effective with other first responders when I was training them in resilience and mental health. For example, I referenced the 'eating an elephant' saying mentioned earlier, which is popular among United States Navy SEALs in the context of their strategies for dealing with feelings of being overwhelmed. This metaphor seems to work especially well with first responders—even vegetarians like me!

Anthony smiled and said 'I like that' when I told him how to eat an elephant, and I shared an article with him about this metaphor. He followed up with me days later to relate to me how helpful this perspective on taking things one step at a time had been for him as he sought to view his situation in a more positive light. In the world of neuroscience, positive psychology, and resilience, this approach is referred to as reframing or cognitive reappraisal. The idea is that the situation stays the same in one aspect but individuals alter their perspective, approaches, and actions in order to cope in a more positive manner.

Two other practices that I shared with Anthony I consider to be the foundation of resilience: controlled breathing and gratitude. I offer more on these practices later in the chapter, but here it is enough to say that they helped him to focus on what he could control and to come to terms better with what he could not. After practicing the breathing exercises for a few days, Anthony sent me a message: 'Go figure, breathing works. I been doing it at different points, especially when I am stressed and it helps.'

He also reached out to a psychologist whom he had seen for a while. He was reluctant to do so at first because of concern about being prescribed medication that would impact his duty status. Anthony's reluctance in this regard was understandable since seeking help and taking certain medications can indeed impact the way an officer is treated on the job. Negative consequences can include being placed on restricted duty, reassessment of current assignment status, ineligibility for off-duty employment, and financial strain owing to decreased opportunities for overtime. These are all very real consequences of seeking help, and they cannot be ignored. In the face of Anthony's reluctance, I reminded him of the elephant metaphor, and he agreed to have a conversation with his doctor. This was fortunate, for the alternative was continuing in his downward spiral, including constantly thinking and worrying about catastrophic, worst-case scenarios.

Speaking more generally, I remind my colleagues, and any first responders who care to listen, that we need to be rational when thinking about medications and duty status. If someone is taking a medication with a warning label that cautions against 'operating heavy machinery' while doing so, it may not be appropriate for that person to be carrying their firearm. However, treatment may not include such medications, so the situation is not a reason for doom and gloom; additionally, relinquishing one's firearm in order to receive treatment is neither automatic nor permanent.

I frequently say, 'What we don't know, we don't know,' and this goes for psychiatrists and psychologists, too. What I mean is that it makes sense to inform your mental health professional that you are a first responder and a member of law enforcement so that they can take this fact into account when considering a medication plan that is both helpful and safe—safe for you, your partner, and the community.

Real resilience

The work of first responders is unique in the sense that often, in the midst of another person's chaos, we are expected to 'fix' the problem right away. We are there in others' worst moments, and they look to us to restore a sense of calm. What I have been saying here is that, in order to remain prepared to help others, we must continually look after ourselves. Again, this kind of thinking is smart and strategic. The benefits for us as individuals include the ability to maintain a healthy lifestyle, and those for our agencies include reduced absenteeism and increased effectiveness.

For first responders seeking to become healthier members of the workforce and better human beings, resilience practices are vital. To be realistic, no one set of practices will by itself bring about this kind of improvement. Rather, resilience must be part of a much broader process that includes assessing the policies and procedures in first responders' environments that promote help-seeking, proactive mental and physical health practices, support for staff by leadership, and a view of accountability as a value rather than a form of punishment.

Real resilience, then, does not come about through attending a one-off training session or workshop, reading through a set of tips, or watching a video. Those methods reflect a 'check-box' mentality that is more concerned about protecting agencies from liability than about creating a culture of genuine resiliency.

This is not to say that training sessions and the like do not serve a purpose. They do, and that purpose should be to complement more in-depth practices that are sustainable throughout an officer's career, from training at the academy all the way into retirement. In order to instill resilience in first responders, the message and messenger must be appropriate for this audience, as discussed above, and include realistic and practical measures. Further, these efforts must be supported and utilised by all members of all ranks, both uniformed and civilian, in order to help establish their relevance to and importance for each specific agency.

The following practices have been adapted from the 'warr;or21' resilience program, which was initially designed for law enforcement officers and other first responders but has since been adapted for use by members of the general public.[2] Importantly, these practices have been shown in numerous neuroscience studies to be effective in enhancing resilience and increasing the ability to cope with stressful and traumatic situations in both professional and personal contexts.

This is the essence of neuroplasticity—knowing that the brain is constantly changing in response to experiences rather than becoming permanently fixed or stagnant at a certain age. This concept of neuroplasticity should be reassuring, for it means that individuals have greater control than they might realise over their lives, including the ability to shape their perspectives anew again and again. Therefore, it can be useful to see these practices as laying bricks in a pathway to mental health and resilience. They help in the cultivation of the ability to reframe, cope with, and learn from our experiences rather than walling them off or carrying them around in our rucksack (or backpack) as a burden.

Gratitude

I will be the first to admit that I started off dismissive of gratitude practices. I realised how important that these practices can be when I came across them in book after book and multiple research studies. The fact is that gratitude practices are not going to make a first responder 'soft'. The opposite is true: they make us sharp and help prevent us from becoming bitter and filled with negativity and hate. Gratitude is all about taking time to acknowledge that something good occurs every day, including on seemingly dull and uneventful days and, especially, those that are tough and stressful.

Try it: Write down, each night as close to when you go to sleep, the following: one thing that made you happy that day, one nice thing someone did for you that day, and one nice thing you did for someone that day. Try this out for five days and here is the challenge—don't repeat yourself with any of them. Finally, when writing each down, do not do it hastily to complete it as fast as possible. Take time to reflect on and think about it as it happened and what it felt like.

Controlled breathing

One of the core practices of any resilience program is controlled breathing. This technique can increase focus, calm, and happiness, reduce stress, and improve sleep—which are benefits that anyone can appreciate. There is no trick to controlled breathing and there is no one way to do it. A variety of science-based practices are out there that can be helpful, and the best approach is to try a few out to see what works best for you. One of the reasons that controlled breathing is so important is the reminder it provides that, as much chaos as there may be in your life, you always control your breath. This awareness can, in turn, ease your mind with the knowledge that, if you can control your breath, you can control other things as well.

Try it: Exhale the air from your lungs. Then breathe in through your nose for four seconds and exhale for four more seconds through your nose (eventually try to exhale for six seconds). As you breathe in and out, make sure that your stomach expands and contracts (rather than your chest). Start off doing this exercise for one minute every morning soon after you first wake and work up to five minutes up for a week. Also, keep track of your breathing exercises in a notebook.

Another method is to breathe naturally while concentrating on nothing else. You can try placing a hand on your stomach as you do so. Again, try this exercise at first for one minute every morning soon after waking and work up to five minutes over the course of a week.

Sleep

As has been seen, first responders often have sleep issues, and it is also well known that good sleep is crucial for maintaining positive mental health and resilience. Sleep impacts a person's mood and overall well-being and assists in recovering from stress and trauma. Generally speaking, most people require 7–9 hours of sleep a day. Considering the hectic and unpredictable nature of first responders' schedules, though, realistically, some sleep is better than none, and it is important to try to get the recommended amount on days off.

Try it: Keep a sleep log in the same notebook just mentioned for the breathing exercises. Try it for two weeks, making a record of when you go to bed and when you wake and your total hours of sleep. During this time, try to establish a sleep routine (such as not using electronics in bed) and to get as close to the recommended 7–9 hours as possible.

Cognitive reappraisal

This practice involves finding alternative, positive, meanings for situations that can be labeled negative. It is important to note that this does not mean minimising or disregarding the negative aspects of something that happens; instead, the idea is to reframe it so as to see what good, opportunities, or benefits also came about. The benefits of cognitive reappraisal have been demonstrated in research done with survivors of the Holocaust and the 9/11 terrorist attacks, and first responders are advised to consider this method of 'seeing' things differently.

Try it: Think of a recent time when you 'failed'. Now try to consider it differently than you have in the past by identifying three positive aspects of or outcomes from your 'failure'. Perhaps it led to a better relationship or increased level of trust with someone or to a better approach in a similar situation later; maybe one positive outcome was the fact that you did not give up.

Social connection

Spending time with friends and loved ones is often described as a key element of resilience, especially for first responders. Social connection of this sort helps counter self-isolation. The simple fact is that people are social creatures, and everyone benefits from the company of positive people who appreciate each other. There is nothing 'soft' about seeking out social connections, either. For first responders, socialising counters negative thoughts that people do not like us, that only bad things are happening, that no one understands us, and that we are hopeless and helpless. The company of others in a safe environment helps us get through the tough moments.

Try it: Make sure to spend time with family or friends as often as possible, and make a special effort to talk about things that you enjoy outside of work. Also, avoid consuming too much alcohol, or for that matter, any alcohol at all; don't let alcohol be the reason to get together, but rather the company. Try to incorporate some fun activities, such as coffee or a meal, working out, going for a walk or run, or even watching a funny show or movie, into your time spent with others.

Purpose

It is often helpful to identify goals, both short- and long-term. Also, remind yourself of how your work is serving a greater purpose, one beyond yourself that benefits the community. Purpose involves looking past your work and checking in with yourself by asking about the 'why' in your life.

Try it: Identify a long-term goal and then connect to it some short-term goals that you can achieve starting tomorrow and the next day in order to progress towards it. Then, reflect on why this long-term goal is important to you and how it will help both you and others.

Realistic optimism

Everyone should understand that hard, purposeful work increases the potential of—but does not guarantee—success and rewards. Additionally, in order to increase the chances of positive outcomes, strategic practice and action are needed.

Try it: Think about some recent successes that you have achieved. Then reflect on the hard work, grit, determination, and dedication that this achievement required. Though the positive outcomes were not guaranteed, you demonstrated some of your positive qualities and observed the positive results that are possible. Try this reflection on your successes on two consecutive Sunday nights.

Positivity

This practice is similar to many of those mentioned above, but it involves looking at your efforts and reminding yourself of all that you are doing to look after yourself. If you have been enduring tough, negative experiences, this practice serves as a reminder that you have been taking the time to reflect on what is good.

Try it: After a week of trying the practices suggested above, take some time to reflect on the progress that you have made and how you are putting in the effort to look after yourself and build your mental health and resilience. Think also about the people you surround yourself with and those close to you and whether they are like-minded, positive, and will be there to help you when you need it most.

My reason for sharing these tips and practices is to provide options that have proved to work. Thus, the neuroscience data show that developing and utilising flexibility and resilience can bring about real improvements in mental health. To be effective, resilience practices must be adapted and modified rather than adhering to a one-size-fits-all, cookie-cutter design approach. The consistent application of these practices that is necessary to 're-wire' the brain cannot be achieved when there is only one tool in the resilience toolbox.

Conclusion

No-one forced us to work as first responders. We came to this job voluntarily, but we did not know that we were also often putting ourselves at risk for developing mental health conditions. We did not expect to get an increased risk of mental health conditions, to work in a system that stigmatises mental health, to be called racists and have vile things screamed at us during 'peaceful' protests, to endure endless sleepless nights and fractured family relationships, or to feel driven to self-medicate with alcohol and prescription drugs.

Personal resilience practices, however, can remind us about our unique perspective as first responders as well as the control that we have over our lives. In the face of all kinds of adversity, a resilient outlook can help us to realise that the situation is not hopeless and that we are not helpless. We are not alone, either, and a big part of resilience is reaching out. Just as we have the backing of our brothers and sisters when we are out on the streets, we need to be able to rely on the first responder community when we are experiencing stress, anxiety, trauma, and other hardships.

Readers are invited to take what they can from the stories shared in this chapter. As always and once again, perspective is crucial. From my perspective, these stories and suggestions illuminate a pathway of recovery and hope. We all have resilience in us, make no mistake about it. Let us continue working on enhancing our resilience and ensuring that we have in place coping strategies that promote mental health. After all, as protectors, guardians, and warriors, taking care of ourselves is not selfish; it is both wise and well-deserved.

Onward, together.

Endnotes

1   The identifying details of individuals and agencies have been changed or omitted in order to protect the anonymity of those involved.

2   These practices are shared for informational purposes and are not intended as a substitute for consulting a licensed healthcare professional.

9 Mitigating risk factors and building protective factors as prevention strategies

Katy Kamkar and Konstantinos Papazoglou

Presenting the issue

Clinical depression, anxiety disorders, trauma, and stressor-related disorders, in particular, post-traumatic stress disorder (PTSD), together with substance use disorders are among the many mental health conditions increasingly being identified and addressed as part of workplace mental health prevention and interventions. Depression is the third highest cause of the burden of disease and is predicted to be the leading cause of disease burden in 2030 (World Health Organisation, 2008). Prevention and early interventions are essential given negative outcomes resulting from common mental health conditions left untreated and for a prolonged period of time (World Health Organisation, 2001).

One of the many pathways to build and optimise prevention involves interventions at both individual and organisational levels—creating a healthy positive organisational culture and improving workplace mental health promotion by reducing workplace risk factors and identifying and building individual as well organisational strengths and protective factors. Occupational stressors can increase the risk of mental health conditions, both at clinical and sub-clinical levels, including depression, anxiety disorders, burnout, and psychological distress (such as Memish, Martin, Bartlett, Dawkins, & Sanderson, 2017; Harvey et al., 2017; Joyce et al., 2016) both at individual and organisational levels (for example, Memish, Martin, Bartlett, Dawkins, & Sanderson, 2017; Martin, Karanika-Murray, Biron, & Sanderson, 2014). Analogously, both potential traumatic events and occupational stressors (organisational stressors and operational stressors) have been found to be associated with mental health conditions and with occupational stressors being significant contributors after controlling for traumatic exposure (see Carleton et al., 2020).

The integral role of prevention
In an international review of guidelines on workplace mental health by Memish, Martin, Bartlett, Dawkins, & Sanderson (2017), the key themes included:

1. taking an integrated approach to workplace mental health;
2. interventions are preventative when risk factors related to work are modified or minimised; protective factors are promoted and illnesses are managed; and
3. prevention approaches, primary, secondary and tertiary, must occur at both worker and organisation-level factors (LaMontagne et al., 2007; LaMontagne et al., 2014).

Any education and mental health promotion and interventions at primary prevention would lead to the most effective outcome when carried out along with secondary and tertiary prevention with interventions at both worker and organisations levels (e.g., Memish, Martin, Bartlett, Dawkins, & Sanderson, 2017; Giga, Noblet, Faragher, & Cooper, 2003; LaMontagne et al., 2007b).

Prevention involves any kind of intervention aimed at preventing the onset, recurrence, severity, and impact of health conditions. Primary prevention is aimed towards reducing the onset or likelihood of an illness. It generally involves building resilience through a two-step process: reducing risk factors and building protective factors. Any proactive education and mental health promotion can fall within the primary prevention care, such as online resilience training. Secondary prevention involves any interventions aimed at identifying and addressing health problems at an early stage, such as screening tests. Tertiary prevention care involves evidence-based treatment and interventions, and disability management, such as evidence-based cognitive behavioural treatment with work interventions, aimed at reducing disability and improving overall functioning and return to work. Any interventions that are provided at secondary and, or, tertiary prevention care can also be included within primary prevention care, including for instance, peer support, ways of accessing resources to care, the need for any work modification or accommodation, learning problem solving skills, and proactive and healthy coping strategies to cope with life or work stressors.

Barriers to service use and pathways to care

Mental health conditions are associated with the loss of productivity (Birnbaum et al., 2010). In fact, research findings suggest that workers experiencing depression are more productive when receiving treatment than workers with depression who are not receiving treatment (Dewa, Thompson, Jacobs, 2011). Mojtabai and colleagues (2011) identified three types of mental health service use barriers, including not recognising that help is needed, structural factors, for example, financial concerns; whether services are available, and attitudinal factors, for example, stigma; wanting to cope with the health condition independently by questioning the efficacy of treatment. In addition, they found that attitudinal barriers, in particular, wanting to cope with the illness independently, are the most common and frequent type of barriers to seeking treatment, rather than structural barriers (Mojtabai et al., 2011).

In a study by Dewa and Hoch (2015), researchers tried to look at the impacts on work productivity of three types of barriers to mental health service use, with the goal of targeting interventions to increase service use. They found that the largest reduction in productivity loss occurs when all three service use barriers are removed, that is not recognising when help is needed, structural factors and attitudinal factors. Specifically, among a population-based survey of Canadian workers, they found that removing the service need recognition barrier is associated with a 33 percent decrease in work productivity losses. There is, however, a 49 percent decrease in productivity loss when all three mental health service use barriers are removed.

The authors recommend a collaboration among government, health care systems, and employers in order to help overcome barriers to care. Taken together, prevention and intervention efforts towards building awareness of mental health symptoms and stigma reduction, are indicated. The findings also show that a comprehensive system strategy needs to include:

- collaboration among all stakeholders;
- the need for education and for any learning to be translated into work and practiced;

- prevention at primary, secondary and tertiary levels of continuum of care;
- interventions at both worker and organisational levels; and
- ensuring access to resources and treatment and case management and disability management for return to work, better prognosis and recovery, and work productivity.

Mental health risk factors

Building pathways to resilience involve strategies and interventions aimed at reducing risk factors at both individual levels and organisational levels (for example, Harvey et al., 2017; Memish Martin, Bartlett, Dawkins, & Sanderson, 2017). A comprehensive strategy to workplace mental health entails identifying and assessing multiple risk factors, including burnout and mental health disorders, as well as occupational stressors, including organisational and operational stressors, work demands, work resources, workplace culture and leadership. A comprehensive understanding of sources of stress help towards optimal education, prevention and interventions, optimal treatment interventions and return to work, and strengthening resiliency pathways at both organisational and worker levels.

Burnout

Burnout has been found to have an adverse impact on health and work performance (see, for example, Borritz et al., 2010; Fragoso et al., 2016). Burnout is characterised by exhaustion, depersonalisation or cynicism, and lack of professional efficacy (Maslach, Jackson, & Leiter, 1996). The experience of exhaustion is often emotional, psychological, and physical, often marked with elevated fatigue, low energy, and insomnia. There is growing cynicism toward the value of one's occupation and ability to complete job duties and elevated fatigue resulting from work demands (Maslach, Jackson, & Leiter, 1996). The depersonalisation or cynicism can lead to emotional numbness or feeling emotionally distant from one's work, reduced interest in activities, losing motivation or interest in what was once a passion and/or reduced care. Reduced professional efficacy is associated with low self-confidence, low self-efficacy where one is doubting their capability of performing their work to the best of their ability, negative views of self and negative self-evaluation.

One can view burnout as a loss and grief given the emotional numbness related to the self, loss of identity and loss of self-confidence, loss of motivation or one's added value to work. The exhaustion component of burnout has also been found to result from an imbalance between job demands and job resources (Bianchi, Schonfeld, & Laurent, 2015). A systematic review and meta-analysis by Koutsimani, Montgomery, & Georganta (2019) looking at the relationship between burnout, depression, and anxiety found no conclusive overlap between burnout and depression and between burnout and anxiety. The results indicated that they are all different constructs. Hence, the need for prevention and interventions efforts to include all the above constructs to ensure a comprehensive approach is taken.

In a one-year longitudinal study, both job demands and job resources were found to predict burnout and symptoms of depression over time (Hatch, Potter, Martus, Rose, & Freude, 2019), while also being associated with symptoms of depression independent from burnout. The authors found evidence that both burnout and symptoms of depression change in the same direction and that no construct has a stronger temporal relation over the other. They also found that employee's mental health need to include assessment of burnout, depression symptoms and job-related stressors.

Compassion fatigue[1]
The occupational demands associated with the work of first responders often involves officers being exposed to individuals who have been hurt, abused, injured, or even killed. First responders' work is clearly an occupation that is characterised by dangerous and distressing incidents (Burke & Mikkelsen, 2007; Crank, 2004; Cross & Ashley, 2004; Karlsson & Christianson, 2003; Kelley, 2005; Violanti, Castellano, O'Rourke, & Paton, 2006; Waters & Ussery, 2007). The foundation of first responders' work includes serving and pro-tecting with calls ranging from monotonous to life-threatening (Cross & Ashley, 2004; Henry, 2004; Papazoglou, Koskelainen, McQuerrey Tuttle, & Pitel, 2017; Slate, Johnson, & Colbert, 2007; Violanti, Castellano, O'Rourke, & Paton, 2006; Waters & Ussery, 2007; Weiss et al., 2010). First responders are regularly exposed to critical incidents, such as motor vehicle accidents and fatalities, cases of abuse and mistreatment of vulnerable populations, dealing with violent subjects, that can have long-lasting effects on their overall mental health (Cross & Ashley, 2004; Karlsson & Christianson, 2003). It is not a normal condition for the human brain to be exposed to human misery at the heightened levels experienced by many first responders. In addition, sustained and continuous exposure to stress and critical incidents

can contribute to declining mental function (Heim & Nemeroff, 2009). This is particularly worrying given that mental functioning is a necessity in this type of work. First responders must enter a career with exceptional mental health and are expected to remain that way for the duration of their careers.

The cost of caring (Figley, 1995) among Red Cross workers, nurses, doctors, and other caregivers, who themselves often become victim to secondary traumatic stress disorder (STSD) among first responders, is seen in the form of compassion fatigue. It can have adverse effects on the physical, emotional, and mental health of first responders, which is directly and indirectly related to overall work performance (Andersen & Papazoglou, 2015). Seeing the worst parts of society, along with caring for victims, can negatively influence job performance. For example, first responders may misplace aggression and anger in the form of excessive use of force issues and citizen complaints, both of which can lead to liability issues. In addition to job performance concerns, officers may struggle on a personal level both physically and mentally when combatting compassion fatigue. First responders are skilled at concealing their emotions such that others may be unaware that something is happening in the officer's life until problematic behaviour surfaces.

First responders are often reluctant to admit that they may be struggling, especially with mental health issues (Olson & Wasilewski, 2016). Issues that can affect one's mental and emotional health often carry a stigma, even more so within subcultures like law enforcement (Violanti, Owens, McCanlies, Fekedulegn, & Andrew, 2018; Workman-Stark, 2017). First responders' professional culture influences how incidents are framed and how they are perceived by officers (Waters & Ussery, 2007). First responders' feelings of reluctance towards mental health improvement programs exemplifies the dark side of first responders' culture where seeking help is stigmatised as weakness (Hohner, 2017; Workman-Stark, 2017). Hohner (2017) adds that first responders are worried about peer support programs backfiring, as they fear that their expression of concerns and negative experiences might be conveyed to management. Additionally, availability and accessibility to mental health resources within agencies may prevent first responders from receiving the help they need (Violanti, Mnatsakanova, Burchfiel, Hartley, & Andrew, 2012). Generally, first responders that expressed job dissatisfaction due to organisational and departmental factors were more likely to experience symptoms of depression, anxiety and traumatic stress (Gershon, Barocas, Canton, Xianbin Li, & Vlahov, 2009).

First responders play a key role in critical incidents that constitute a vital protective factor that is critical in shifting the victims' lives away from a trajectory towards poor, long-term outcomes (Akers & Kaukinen, 2009; Garrett, 2004; Marans, Smolover, & Hahn, 2012; Marans & Hahn, 2017). When properly equipped, police officers may simultaneously play a critical role in advancing victims' recovery from traumatic experiences while more broadly contributing to the strengthening of relationships between agencies and communities (Akers & Kaukinen, 2009; Manzella & Papazoglou, 2014; Marans & Hahn, 2017). In this context, 'compassion satisfaction' (Stamm, 2002), refers to the return that caregiving professionals derive from helping those who suffer. Research has also shown that a considerable number of police officers do not appear to value the importance of their services in the communities they serve (Papazoglou, 2017). While these first responders still serve their communities, their inability to view their work as valuable increases the likelihood that they will approach their duties in a perfunctory manner ('just the facts ma'am'). In other situations, first responders may suppress their emotions or be emotionally disengaged because their attention is solely focused on investigation-related aspects of the incident and they fail to appreciate the value of additional, trauma-informed approaches that may not only be critically helpful to victims and witnesses but also strengthening their contributions to the investigative process itself.

Recent research has indicated that frontline professionals who experience compassion satisfaction feel a greater sense of success and increased motivation because they are able to appreciate the value their services add to the lives of the individuals and the communities they serve (Papazoglou, 2017). In addition, other studies have concluded that police officers with high levels of compassion satisfaction tend to show greater job performance, more commitment to their duties, and higher levels of self-perceived wellbeing.

Perhaps unsurprisingly, research has revealed that compassion satisfaction is negatively associated with compassion fatigue. Essentially, an increase in compassion fatigue appears to be associated with a decrease in compassion satisfaction and the reverse. One possible explanation for this relationship may be that compassion fatigue symptoms, such as feeling overwhelmed or being hypervigilant and irritable, may preclude officers from experiencing compassion satisfaction. Although more research is required in order to substantiate this negative association, it seems clear that frontline professionals with high levels of compassion satisfaction are able to appreciate the importance of their services despite being exposed to overwhelming experiences as a result of caring for trauma victims in the line of duty. In addition, the negative association between compassion fatigue and compassion satisfaction indicates that using various techniques to strengthen compassion satisfaction can mitigate or entirely neutralise the virulent experience of compassion fatigue.

Individual first responders have varying reactions when exposed to traumatic or potentially traumatic incidents. Those who may have a negative reaction to an incident will often refuse to come forward, for fear of what their peers may think. This leaves many first responders suffering in silence. The repression of emotions among police officers has been associated with poor health holistically (Wastell, 2002), and those who suffer in silence may revert to maladaptive coping mechanisms, such as the use of drugs and/or alcohol abuse to try to deal with their stress and trauma (Cross & Ashley, 2004; Hackett & Violanti, 2003; Violanti & Samuels, 2007; Waters & Ussery, 2007). Asking for help in police work is difficult for many first responders because they fear doing so could cost their career, livelihood, and the respect of fellow officers. An occupation that operates at societal extremes reiterates the necessity to reinforce such cultural beliefs (Crank, 2004; Karlsson & Christianson, 2003; Kelley, 2005).

The impact of compassion fatigue on first responders' health and wellbeing is one side of the spectrum. Alternatively, it should be considered that compassion fatigue is very likely to affect officers' performance at work. Trauma scholars mentioned that caregiving professionals may even experience dissociation during their work with traumatised individuals (Danieli, 1996). Mathieu (2007) suggests that while each individual may express certain unique symptoms of compassion fatigue, those entering the danger zone of compassion fatigue may show warning signs of 'intrusive imagery or dissociation.' Healthcare professionals experiencing compassion fatigue have often felt that they were 'frequently dissociated [and] walked around in an altered state' (Babbel, 2012). Similarly, police officers support numerous victims of crimes, accidents, or natural catastrophes over the course of their career. Compassion fatigue may, therefore, create ripple effects of poor health and mental malfunctioning. Research has shown that those who suffer from previous mental health challenges are more likely to develop PTSD in the experience of a life-threatening situation (McFarlane, 2000; Sayed, Iacoviello, & Charney, 2015).

First responders' personal and family lives are also impacted by compassion fatigue (Sprang, Clark, & Whitt-Woosley, 2007). At the end of their shift, first responders return back to their homes where their families are waiting for them. There, they assume the role of a parent, spouse, sibling and friend. Officers who suffer from police compassion fatigue may become cynical, apathetic, negative, and aloof which could negatively influence their interactions with family and friends (Cox, Marchionna, & Fitch, 2017; Fuller, 2003). As a result, a snowball phenomenon may occur and mundane or minor family or personal issues may remain unresolved and aggravate over time until they lead to family discord or potential divorce (Miller, 2007).

Moral injury[2]

The idea of moral injury has been pervasive in human societies for thousands of years and perhaps even since the existence of humankind. In the Greco-Roman tradition, warrior narratives reference the experience of moral conflicts on the battlefield, called miasma or μίασμα—moral pollution and purification, defining it as a situation wherein someone with legitimate and recognised authority betrays what is right in a critical situation (Shay, 2014). In the modern era, conceptualisation of moral injury first flowed from research and clinical work with American military personnel and veterans. It became apparent through both research and clinical practice that veterans who served in combat zones were exposed to traumas that altered their moral beliefs and values systems. In effect, some veterans experienced a violation of their morals or beliefs during their service and became skeptical about whether or not the world is a just, benevolent and safe place. Thereby, a formal definition refers to moral injury as exposure to unprecedented traumatic life events wherein one perpetrates, fails to prevent, or witnesses actions that 'transgress deeply held moral beliefs and expectations' (Litz et al., 2009, p. 1). Similarly, the United States Marine Corps uses the term 'inner conflict' when referring to experiences involving moral injury (Nash & Litz, 2013). Inner conflict may occur not only when a Marine experiences extraordinary violence, such as terrorists using children as 'human shields', but also in moments when they are ordered to abandon a wounded comrade to save their own lives.

Events that may lead to moral injury include handling or uncovering human remains, the inability to render help to severely wounded victims, involvement in friendly fire incidents, being present when non-combatants are harmed or killed by accident, witnessing others injure or kill unnecessarily without intervening to stop their actions, or observing war-related destruction of property, and killing enemy soldiers (Drescher et al., 2011; Frankfurt & Frazier, 2016; Litz et al., 2009). These experiences are labeled transgressive acts to identify them as potentially traumatic experiences distinct from the fear-based traumas associated with posttraumatic stress disorder. The goal of this article was to review empirical and clinical data relevant to transgressive acts and moral injury, to identify gaps in the literature, and to encourage future research and interventions. We reviewed literature on the three broad arms of the moral injury model proposed by Litz and colleagues (2009). These experiences violate an individual's moral belief systems and share core features of guilt and shame for having been involved in these events.

Moral injury and police wellbeing

The experience of moral injury carries negative physical and psychological effects for officers. Moral injury, although not recognised as a mental health disorder within the fifth edition of the *Diagnostic and Statistical Manual of Mental Disorders* (DSM-5) (American Psychiatric Association, 2013), can lead to lasting emotional and psychological impact. It is, therefore, a significant mental health issue that needs to be recognised during mental health assessment for a more comprehensive case conceptualisation. It must be kept in mind throughout treatment interventions and become an essential part of evidence-based education around mental health prevention and promotion. Moral injury has been associated with intrusion, avoidance and arousal symptoms of PTSD (Feinstein, Pavisian, & Storm, 2018), depression, suicidal ideation and anger (Bryan, Bryan, Morrow, Etienne, & Ray-Sannerud, 2014; Gaudet, Sowers, Nugent, & Boriskin, 2016) and, as discussed earlier, with the onset of guilt and shame (Nazarov et al., 2015). Taking a broader perspective approach also helps to further understand the impact of moral injury and related diagnoses such as post-traumatic stress disorder (PTSD) or depression, which are part of what has been referred to as 'Operational Stress Injuries' (OSI).

Initially conceptualised within the Canadian Armed Forces (Standing Senate Committee on National Security and Defence, 2015), OSI includes any persistent psychological difficulties resulting from operational or service-related duties. Common mental health problems at the core of OSI includes PTSD, anxiety disorders, depression, substance use disorders, suicidal ideation or any other conditions that may interfere with a person's level of functioning, personal, social or occupational. Stressors related to employment, finances, family, relationships as well as pain and physical health issues and changes within role or identity can all be part of OSI which, in turn, causes further pain, suffering and impaired functioning.

OSI, and in particular trauma, can shatter an individual's core belief system through fundamental changes to a person's views of themselves, others, the world and the future. How events, circumstances or situations are perceived, interpreted or viewed can drastically change following traumatic events and frequently reflect elements of moral injury. A changed worldview can lead to potential difficulty regulating emotions, experiencing intense mixed and negative emotions, difficulty making healthy decisions and taking proactive strategies, difficulty resuming regular work duties, decreased work productivity, reduced self-efficacy at work, and feeling incompetent. Over time, any future events or situations will tend to be filtered through the lens that has been altered, thus, further compounding suffering and impaired functioning.

Individual responses vary between officers, depending on how each person processes events or circumstances. What may set in motion a fundamental change in one individual may have an entirely different effect on another individual, or possibly even no impact. This makes understanding, recognising, and treating OSI far more difficult compared to physical injuries experienced by officers.

While most attention has been given to emotions such as anxiety and fear resulting from traumatic incidents that police officers have often faced in line of duty, other emotions such as guilt and shame have received much less attention despite their contributions to health and work outcomes (for example, Wright & Gudjonsson, 2007; Cohen, Wolf, Panter, & Insko, 2011). Mixed emotions related to guilt and shame often result in internal conflict within the self where actions of self or others do not harmonise with one's moral values, standards, beliefs or conscience. Guilt and shame are related to maintaining and exacerbating psychopathology, interpersonal conflict, self-isolation and avoidance, disruption in work activities, prolonged recovery, and present a significant barrier to personal, social and occupational functioning.

First responders often report difficulty with resuming their regular work activities or with the return to process after a period of absence as a result of feeling ashamed, or not wanting to go out to public places or attending social events out of fear of seeing people or colleagues due to guilt or shame. Those emotions can lead at times to more self-isolation and prominent avoidance than other emotions, such as fear or anxiety.

Other types of moral distress

In addition to the risk for moral injury presented by operational stressors already discussed, such as shooting an unarmed someone after initially believing they possessed a firearm and witnessing horrific crime scenes, organisational stressors can also present risk for moral distress. Common organisational stressors related to job stress and burnout (Cooper & Marshall, 1976; Finney, Stergiopoulos, Hensel, Bonato, & Dewa, 2013) include stressors intrinsic to the job; one's role in an organisation and its system of punishments and rewards; supervisory relationships, administrative structures and workplace culture. Organisational stressors can lead to first responders feeling they have little or no control over their work. For example, just being 'along for the ride' may be a common sentiment among those experiencing organisational stressors.

In the work of first responders, risk for moral injury related to organisational stressors can commonly occur and be compounded by excessive work demands that are difficult to manage; limited opportunities for training and limited resources; heavy workloads; lack of support; dissatisfaction around one's role in the organisation; role ambiguity or the role not fitting one's abilities or aptitudes; unclear responsibilities and vague perogatives; strained relationships with supervisors; unresolved interpersonal conflicts; harassment and bullying in the workplace; or lack of perceived organisational support following highly publicised and potentially controversial incidents. When first responders are unable to pursue what they believe or perceive to be the right plan of action or decision, or fail to meet their own expectations due to, for instance, work related obstacles, interpersonal conflicts, and limited resources or circumstances beyond their control, they may subsequently feel guilty, demoralised and/or helpless. Any of the stressors named above can lead to internal conflict or transgression of one's moral values and belief system and, in turn, set the stage for moral injury.

'Moral distress' is also related to a variety of other emotional, psychological, and physiological reactions such as sleep disturbance, bad dreams, appetite changes, feelings of worthlessness, reduced sense of self-confidence, and headaches (Fry, Harvey, Hurley, & Foley, 2002). The emotional and psychological impact of moral distress can also over time increase the risk for burnout (Fumis, Amarante, Nascimento, & Junior, 2017). Traumatic incidents noted above, including operational and organisational stressors, can lead not only to trauma reactions that are fear-based or trauma reactions that are loss-based, but also to moral injury-based trauma reactions (Gray et al., 2012; Held, Klassen, Brennan, & Zalta, 2018; Litz, Lebowitz, Gray, & Nash, 2016) especially in combat situations—thus, morally injurious events are often implicated in the development of posttraumatic stress disorder (PTSD.

Trauma reactions that are fear-based can include fear for safety of self or others following increased violence and increased likelihood of assault or gang related incidents. They can also include fear of impending doom; worries of something bad happening to self or others; and anxiety being in social situations or in public places and witnessing interpersonal conflicts or arguments. Trauma reactions that are loss-based can include, for instance, losing a colleague to suicide; death of a colleague following a shooting incident; or a death scene that resembled an officer's personal life possibly involving a child of same age or a house resembling one's own home. For moral injury-based trauma reactions, the symptoms can be similar to OSI symptoms and may include mixed emotions such as feelings of shame, guilt, remorse, or anger; irritability, negative beliefs about oneself; self-blame; avoidance and self-isolation; withdrawal from social situations; distressing intrusive memories of traumatic incidents and related nightmares; difficulties with sleep; and difficulties with concentration and making decisions. The symptoms related to moral injury can also contribute to maintenance and/or exacerbation of psychological disorders related to OSI.

Taken together, building awareness of the harmful impact of moral injury, providing education around moral injury, and recognising the signs and symptoms of moral injury can inform prevention initiatives and contribute to resilience building among officers. It can also help optimise treatment interventions to improve quality of life and well-being, and personal and occupational functioning. At the organisational level, creating healthy culture, providing a people-oriented culture and people focused leadership, building organisational capacities and resources, and implementing psychological health and safety strategies to alleviate organisational stressors could help reduce the risk of moral injury.

Plainly, morally injurious experiences are highly prevalent in first responders' work. Current scholarly literature shows that moral injury violates the moral belief system of the individual, leading to negative and distressing views of self, others, and the world. It also results in a host of negative emotional reactions with guilt and shame as predominant emotions experienced. Taken together, moral injury can have a virulent impact on first responders' health, wellbeing, and overall functioning. Nevertheless, emphasis should be placed on the fact that moral injury is not an inevitable condition. When addressed early, or through prevention, the negative impact of moral injury on officers can be reduced. It is possible that first responders may be inclined to employ unhealthy ways of coping, such as turning to alcohol, relying on isolation or succumbing to cynicism, to battle moral injury symptoms as a desperate way to prevent the negative impact of moral injury in their lives. On many occasions, first responders may not be familiar with healthy ways of coping or preventative strategies to protect themselves against the incapacitating impact of moral injury.

The existing research on first responders and moral injury is more exploratory than explanatory. But as suggested, first responders and scholars can translate military moral injury knowledge into first responders' work to ensure police officers become more cognisant of moral injury in their work. Applying the findings of moral injury research to first responders' work requires a synergistic effort drawing on the goodwill of police leaders, police clinicians, police families and serving police officers. It is essential that the possibility of moral conflict is addressed at the organisational level within police departments. When moral injury is openly addressed in an unapologetic and de-stigmatising way, first responders will feel more comfortable talking about their experience of moral distress. Such dialogue should take place during department meetings because they are facilitated in a collective context in which officers have the opportunity to get feedback from their colleagues and supervisors. This would allow for early signs of moral injury or any inner conflict to be verbalised and processed within a supportive context.

Analogously, first responders' moral dilemmas and conflicts should be addressed during police training and, hence, incorporated into police training curricula. We suggest that first responders' training should encompass the different nuances of critical incidents—such as moral dilemmas, stress levels, decision making, use of force—and that these kinds of incidents should not be approached solely from an operational perspective. Moral injury can potentially affect first responders' capacity for decision making during critical moments, such as when to respond with lethal force, and affect their clarity of judgment in the line of duty. First responders' trainers should encourage first responders to share any moral dilemmas they experience during training so that they are best prepared for real life situations of police work where moral dilemmas and conflicts are both inevitable and unavoidable.

The role of clinicians in preventing and treating moral injury is vital. Clinicians may collaborate with officers who are part of peer support units and help them identify peers who struggle with moral injury, moral conflicts, and moral dilemmas. In addition, clinical treatment, especially in regards to stress and trauma, should explore any morally injurious symptoms experienced by first responders who participate in treatment. Assessing for moral injury allows treatment to address the holistic needs of first responders. Often, issues experienced by first responders in the past have remained unaddressed or ignored because the severity of such issues was undervalued or understudied. In addition, clinicians may guide and encourage first responders to practice strategies that can help them prevent the impact of moral injury in their lives. For instance, prior research with veterans has shown that volunteerism, journaling, mindfulness, and gratitude letters are some ways that can help first responders express their moral conflicts while engaging in activities where they can realise that the world has potential for kindness and fairness and not just violence and unfairness.

Psychological health and safety in the workplace should include education around moral injury in first responders' work as well as increased efforts to reduce likelihood of moral injury or moral distress resulting from operational or organisational stressors. Further research, education, and training are needed to better identify all aspects of moral injury in the first responders' population and to inform moral injury prevention and intervention.

Mental health promotion and education

Shann, Martin, Chester and Ruddock (2019) studied an online workplace mental health intervention for leaders to help reduce stigma related to depression. Results showed depression related stigma was much lower among leaders who completed the online program than the control group. The authors concluded that strong knowledge or positive attitudes are not sufficient to transfer learning or knowledge into workplace and that other key elements such as the work atmosphere and attitudes, organisational readiness and capability and the political context impact the transfer of learning into workplace.

With stigma identified as the largest barrier to help seeking (Lasalvia et al., 2013), continuous effort and creative strategies need to be delivered for stigma reduction. A meta-analysis (Corrigan, Morris, Michaels, Rafacz, & Rüsch, 2012) on stigma reduction found that both education and contact (having personal contact with someone with a mental health condition) were effective at reducing stigma with contact being more effective. Building pathways to care and treatment include:

- identifying signs and symptoms of psychological distress that are increasing over time and causing functional impairment;
- recognising that help is needed;
- workers feeling safe sharing their experiences and not being afraid of stigma and in particular workplace stigma where they might feel judged, not being considered for promotion or any other opportunities, or not feeling supported during disability leave or after leave of absence;
- deciding to receive treatment and knowledge of effectiveness of treatment;
- access to treatment that is evidence-based and resources with expertise;
- engagement in treatment and benefit from treatment; and
- receiving treatment that includes return to work interventions.

In sum, a system is needed that ensures a collaborative care model that helps to increase therapy outcome, positive prognosis, increases overall functioning, in particular occupational functioning and the likelihood of return to work and work productivity and recovery.

Protective factors

Healthy and proactive coping is known to be a protective factor against negative health outcomes following traumatic events and a further contributor to resiliency and well-being (see, for example, Galatzer-Levy, Burton, & Bonanno, 2012; Feder et al., 2013). As discussed earlier, workplace mental health needs to involve increases in protective factors as part of resiliency. To this end, coping flexibility is the ability to utilise flexibility different coping strategies in a particular situation (Bonanno, Pat-Horenczyk, & Noll, 2011) and has been found to be associated with lower levels of post-traumatic stress and depressive symptoms after controlling for co-morbid symptoms, age and time since the traumatic event (Park, Chang, & You, 2015). The authors of those studies found that lower coping flexibility was associated with higher PTSD symptoms as the number of traumatic events increased, with conclusion that coping flexibility is a protective factor for PTSD and depression and the risk for mental health conditions following a series of traumas is higher with lower coping flexibility.

Similarly, Dahm and colleagues (2015) have researched modifiable factors that are related to PTSD and functional impairment to optimise interventions and to that effect studied mindfulness and self-compassion. They looked at the relation of both mindfulness and self-compassion with PTSD symptom severity and disability in veterans. Both mindfulness and self-compassion have been found to be negatively associated with PTSD symptom severity and functional disability, even after controlling for PTSD symptom severity. The findings indicated that prevention and interventions aimed at building mindfulness and self-compassion can help towards reducing the functional disability related to PTSD. Mindfulness involves regulating emotion and atten-tion in the moment and present time by identifying thoughts and emotions and looking at them from an objective standpoint to help reframing thoughts and put them into perspective (see Teasdale et al., 2002). Self-compassion involves being mindful of one's suffering and thoughts and emotions and putting them into perspective, self-kindness and providing self with support and a sense of humanity by acknowledging that everyone is human. Of course, no-one is perfect, all humans make mistakes and suffering is part of the human condition (for instance, Neff, 2003; Neff, 2012).

Sprang, Ford, Kerig, & Bride (2019) observed that an expert panel defined 'Secondary Traumatic Stress' (STS) as a construct that is directly related to, or very closely parallels, the components of PTSD as defined in DSM-5—re-experiencing symptoms of trauma; avoidance related symptoms; alternations in mood and cognitions; and arousal symptoms. They also pointed to an additional domain likely to reflect changes in personal and professionals systems of meaning and beliefs that might result from other stress reactions such as moral distress, reduced empathy or professional self-efficacy. Compassion satisfaction that refers to the satisfaction and gratification that one feels after helping others (Stamm, 2010) has also been found to be a protective factor. To this end, compassion satisfaction has been found to be negatively related to secondary traumatic stress and burnout as well as a likely protective factor against those health risk factors (Simon, Pryce, Roff, & Klemmack, 2006). More recently, Cummings, Singer, Hisaka, & Benuto (2018) found that burnout is a strong predictor of vicarious trauma and secondary traumatic stress. Conversely, compassion satisfaction might be a protective factor against experiencing both. They highlighted the importance of prevention and interventions to reduce burnout and increase compassion satisfaction.

✶ ✶ ✶ ✶

This chapter has highlighted many of the pathways to building workplace mental health and resiliency at both individual and organisational level factors. We looked at workplace risk factors as well workplace strengths and protective factors. When taken together, we believe there is a compelling case for improving mental health education, prevention, and interventions at both individual and organisational levels to produce a positive organisational culture that will enrich individual performance and enhance organisational effectiveness.

References

Akers, C., & Kaukinen, C. (2009). The police reporting behavior of intimate partner violence victims, *Journal of Family Violence, 24*(3), 159–171.

American Psychiatric Association. (2013). *Diagnostic and Statistical Manual of Mental Disorders, 5th Edition. New York American Psychiatric Press Inc.* American Psychiatric Publishing, Inc. https://doi.org/10.1176/appi.books.9780890425596.893619.

Andersen, J. P., & Papazoglou, K. (2015). Compassion fatigue and compassion satisfaction among police officers: An understudied topic. *International Journal of Emergency Mental Health and Human Resilience, 17*(3), 661–663. https://doi.org/10.4172/1522–4821.1000259.

Babbel, S. (2012). Compassion fatigue: Bodily symptoms of empathy. Retrieved from https://www.psychologytoday.com/ca/blog/somatic-psychology/201207/compassion-fatigue.

Bianchi, R., Schonfeld, I. S., & Laurent, E. (2015). Burnout-depression overlap: A review. Clinical Psychology Review, 36, 28—41. http://dx .doi.org/10.1016/j.cpr.2015.01.004.

Birnbaum, H. G., Kessler, R. C., Kelley, D., Ben-Hamadi, R., Joish, V. N., & Greenberg, P. E. (2010). Employer burden of mild, moderate, and severe major depressive disorder: Mental health services utilisation and costs, and work performance. *Depress Anxiety, 27*, 78–89.

Bonanno, G. A., Pat-Horenczyk, R., & Noll, J. (2011). Coping flexibility and trauma: The perceived ability to cope with trauma (PACT) scale. *Psychological Trauma: Theory, Research, Practice, and Policy, 3*, 117–129.

Borritz, M., Christensen, K. B., Bültmann, U., Rugulies, R., Lund, T., Andersen, I., Villadsen, E., Diderichsen, F., & Kristensen, T. S. (2010). Impact of burnout and psychosocial work characteristics on future long-term sickness absence. Prospective results of the Danish PUMA study among human service workers. *Journal of Occupational and Environmental Medicine, 52*(10), 964 –970. http://dx.doi.org/10.1097/JOM.0b013e3181f12f95.

Bryan, A. O., Bryan, C. J., Morrow, C. E., Etienne, N., & Ray-Sannerud, B. (2014). Moral injury, suicidal ideation, and suicide attempts in a military sample. *Traumatology, 20*(3), 154–160. https://doi.org/10.1037/h0099852.

Burke, R. J., & Mikkelsen, A. (2007). Suicidal ideation among police officers in Norway. *Policing: An International Journal of Police Strategies & Management, 30*(2), 228–236. https://doi.org/10.1108/13639510710753234.

Carleton, R. N., Afifi, T. O., Taillieu, T., Turner, S., Mason, J. E., Ricciardelli, R., McCreary, D. R., Vaughan, A. D., Anderson, G. S., Krakauer, R. L., Donnelly, E. A., Camp, R. D., Groll, D., Cramm, H. A., MacPhee, R. A., & Griffiths, C. T. (2020). Assessing the relative impact of diverse stressors among public safety personnel. *International Journal of Environmental Rseearch & Public Health, 17*(4), 1234; https://doi.org/10.3390/ijerph17041234.

Cohen, T. R., Wolf, S. T., Panter, A. T., & Insko, C. A. (2011). Introducing the GASP scale: A new measure of guilt and shame proneness. *Journal of Personality and Social Psychology, 100*(5), 947–966. http://dx.doi.org/10.1037/a0022641.

Cooper, C. L., & Marshall, J. (1976). Occupational sources of stress: a review of the literature relating to coronary heart disease and mental ill health. *Journal of Occupational Psychology, 49*(1), 11–28. https://doi.org/10.1111/j.2044–8325.1976.tb00325.x.

Corrigan, P. W., Morris, S. B., Michaels, P. J., Rafacz, J. D., & Rüsch, N. (2012). Challenging the public stigma of mental illness: A meta-analysis of outcome studies. *Psychiatric Services, 63*, 963–973. http://dx.doi.org/ 10.1176/appi.ps.201100529.

Cox, S. M., Marchionna, S., & Fitch, B. D. (2017). The police culture and work stress. In *Introduction to Policing* (3rd ed., p. 177).

Crank, J. P. (2004). *Understanding Police Culture* (2nd ed.). Cincinnati, OH: Anderson Publishing Co.

Cross, C. L., & Ashley, L. (2004). Police trauma and addiction: Coping with the dangers of the job. *FBI Law Enforcement Bulletin, 73*(10), 24–32. Retrieved from http://www.fbi.gov/stats-services/publications/law-enforcement-bulletin/2013/june/archive.

Cummings, C., Singer, J., Hisaka, R., & Benuto, L. T. (2018). Compassion satisfaction to combat work-related burnout, vicarious trauma, and secondary traumatic stress. *Journal of Interpersonal Violence*, 1–16. DOI: 10.1177/0886260518799502.

Dahm, K., Meyer, E. C., Neff, K., Kimbrel, N. A., Gulliver, S. B., & Morissette, S. B. (2015). Mindfulness, self-compassion, posttraumatic stress disorder symptoms, and functional disability in U. S. Iraq and Afghanistan war veterans. *Journal of Traumatic Stress, 28*(5), 460–464. Doi: 10.1002/jts.22045.

Danieli, Y. (1996). Who takes care of the caregiver? In R. J. Apfel & B. Simon (Eds.), *Minefields in their hearts: The mental health of children in war and communal violence* (pp. 189–205). New Haven, CT: Yale University Press.

Dewa, C. S., Thompson, A. H., & Jacobs, P. (2011). The association of treatment of depressive.

episodes and work productivity. *Canadian Journal Psychiatry, 56*(12), 743–750. doi: 10.1177/070674371105601206.

Dewa, C. S., & Hoch, J. S. (2015). Barriers to mental health service use among workers with depression and work productivity. *Journal of Occupational & Environmental Medicine, 57*(7), 726–731. doi: 10.1097/JOM.0000000000000472.

Drescher, K. D., Foy, D. W., Kelly, C., Leshner, A., Schutz, K., & Litz, B. (2011). An exploration of the viability and usefulness of the construct of moral injury in war veterans. *Traumatology, 17*(1), 8–13. https://doi.org/10.1177/1534765610395615.

Feder, A., Ahmad, S., Lee, E. J., Morgan, J. E., Singh, R., Smith, B. W., Southwick, S. M., & Charney, D. S. (2013). Coping and PTSD symptoms in Pakistani earthquake survivors: Purpose in life, religious coping and social support. *Journal of Affective Disorders, 147*(1–3), 156–163. doi: 10.1016/j.jad.2012.10.027.

Feinstein, A., Pavisian, B., & Storm, H. (2018). Journalists covering the refugee and migration crisis are affected by moral injury not PTSD. *JRSM Open, 9*(3), 1–7. https://doi.org/10.1177/2054270418759010.

Figley, C. R. (1995). *Compassion fatigue: Coping with secondary traumatic stress disorder in those who treat the traumatised. BrunnerMazel psychosocial stress series.* New York, NY: Bruner/Mazel.

Finney, C., Stergiopoulos, E., Hensel, J., Bonato, S., & Dewa, C. S. (2013). Organisational stressors associated with job stress and burnout in correctional officers: A systematic review. *BMC Public Health, 13*(1), 82. https://doi.org/10.1186/1471–2458-13–82.

Fragoso, Z. L., Holcombe, K. J., McCluney, C. L., Fisher, G. G., McGonagle, A. K., & Friebe, S. J. (2016). Burnout and engagement: Relative importance of predictors and outcomes in two health care worker samples. *Workplace Health & Safety, 64*(10), 479—487. http://dx.doi.org/10 .1177/2165079916653414.

Frankfurt, S., & Frazier, P. (2016). A review of research on moral injury in combat veterans. *Military Psychology, 28*(5), 318–330. https://doi.org/10.1037/mil0000132.

Fry, S., Harvey, R., Hurley, A., & Foley, B. (2002). Development of a model of moral distress in military nursing. *Nursing Ethics, 9*(4), 373–387. https://doi. org/10.1191/0969733002ne522oa.

Fuller, M. E. (2003). Living with a cop: A handbook for police officers and their families. Alberta: Lethbridge. Retrieved from https://opus.uleth.ca/bitstream/handle/10133/1150/Fuller_Merle_E.pdf.

Fumis, R. R. L., Amarante, G. A. J., Nascimento, A. F., & Junior, J. M. V. (2017). Moral distress and its contribution to the development of burnout syndrome among critical care providers. *Annals of Intensive Care, 71*(7), 1–8. https://doi.org/10.1186/s13613-017–0293-2.

Galatzer-Levy, I. R., Burton, C. L., & Bonanno, G. A. (2012). Coping flexibility, potentially traumatic life events, and resilience: A prospective study of college student adjustment. *Journal of Social and Clinical Psychology, 31*(6) 542–567. doi.org/10.1521/jscp.2012.31.6.542.

Garrett, P. M. (2004). Talking child protection: The police and social workers "working together." *Journal of Social Work, 4*(1), 77–97. doi.org/10.1177/1468017304042422.

Gaudet, C. M., Sowers, K. M., Nugent, W. R., & Boriskin, J. A. (2016). A review of PTSD and shame in military veterans. *Journal of Human Behavior in the Social Environment, 26*(1), 56–68. doi:10.1080/10911359.2015.1059168.

Gershon, R. R. M., Barocas, B., Canton, A. N., Xianbin Li, L., & Vlahov, D. (2009). Mental, physical, and behavioral outcomes associated with perceived work stress in police officers. *Criminal Justice and Behavior, 36*(3), 275–289. doi:10.1177/0093854808330015.

Giga, S. I., Noblet, A. J., Faragher, B., & Cooper, C. L. (2003). The UK perspective: A review of research on organisational stress management interventions. *Australian Psycholigist, 38*(2), 158–164. doi:10.1080/00050060310001707167.

Gray, M. J., Schorr, Y., Nash, W., Lebowitz, L., Amidon, A., Lansing, A., Maglione, A., Lang, A. J., & Litz, B. T. (2012). Adaptive disclosure: An open trial of a novel exposure-based intervention for service members with combat-related psychological stress injuries. *Behavior Therapy, 43*(2), 407–415. doi:10.1016/j.beth.2011.09.001.

Hackett, D. P., & Violanti, J. M. (2003). *Police suicide: Tactics for prevention.* Springfield, IL:.

Charles C. Thomas.

Harvey, S. B., Modini, M., Joyce, S., Milligan-Saville, J. S., Tan, L., Mykletun, A., Bryant, R. A., Christensen, H., & Mitchell, P. B., (2017). Can work make you mentally ill? A systematic meta-review of work-related risk factors for common mental health problems. *Occupational & Environmental Medicene, 74*(4), 301–310. doi:10.1136/oemed-2016–104015.

Hatch, D. J., Potter, G. G., Martus, P., Rose, U., & Freude, G. (2019). Lagged versus concurrent changes between burnout and depression symptoms and unique contributions from job demands and job resources. *Journal of Occupational Health Psychology, 24*(6), 617–628. doi:10.1037/ocp0000170.

Heim, C., & Nemeroff, C. B. (2009). Neurobiology of posttraumatic stress disorder. *CNS Spectrums, 14*(1 Suppl 1), 13–24.

Held, P., Klassen, B. J., Brennan, M. B., & Zalta, A. K. (2018). Using prolonged exposure and cognitive processing therapy to treat veterans with moral injury-based PTSD: Two case examples. *Cognitive and Behavioral Practice, 25*(3), 377–390. doi:10.1016/j.cbpra.2017.09.003.

Henry, V. E. (2004). *Death work: Police, trauma, and the psychology of survival.* New York, NY: Oxford University Press.

Hohner, C. (2017). *'The environment says it's okay': The tension between peer support and police culture.* Retrieved from https://ir.lib.uwo.ca/etd.

Joyce, S., Modini, M., Christensen, H., Mykletun, A., Bryant, R., Mitchell, P. B., & Harvey, S. B., (2016). Workplace interventions for common mental disorders: A systematic meta-review. *Psychological Medicine, 46*(4), 683–697. doi:10.1017/S0033291715002408.

Karlsson, I., & Christianson, S. (2003). The phenomenology of traumatic experiences in police work. *Policing: An International Journal of Police Strategies & Management, 26*(3), 419–438. doi:10.1108/13639510310489476.

Kelley, T. M. (2005). Mental health and prospective police professionals. *Policing: An International Journal, 28*(1), 6–29. doi:10.1108/13639510510510580959.

Koutsimani, P., Montgomery, A. & Georganta, K. (2019). The relationship between burnout, depression, and anxiety: A systematic review and meta-analysis. *Frontiers in Psychology, 10*(284), 1–19. doi:10.3389/fpsyg.2019.00284.

LaMontagne, A. D., Keegel, T., & Vallance, D. (2007). Protecting and promoting mental health in the workplace: Developing a systems approach to job stress. *Health Promotion Journal of Australia, 18*(3), 221–228. doi:10.1071/HE07221.

LaMontagne, A. D., Martin, A., Page, K. M., Reavley, N. J., Noblet, A. J., Milner, A. J., Keegel, T., & Smith, P. M. (2014). Workplace mental health: Developing an integrated intervention approach. *BMC Psychiatry, 14*(131). doi:10.1186/1471-244X-14-131.

Lasalvia, A., Zoppei, S., Van Bortel, T., Bonetto, C., Cristofalo, D., Wahlbeck, K., Bacle, S. V., Audenhove, C. V., Weeghel, J., Reneses, B., Germanavicius, A., Economou, M., Lanfredi, M., Ando, S., Sartorius, N., Lopez-Ibor, J. J., & Thornicroft, G. (2013). Global pattern of experienced and anticipated discrimination reported by people with major depressive disorder: A cross-sectional survey. *The Lancet, 381*(9860), 55–62. doi:10.1016/S0140-6736(12)61379-8.

Litz, B. T., Lebowitz, L., Gray, M. J., & Nash, W. P. (2016). *Adaptive disclosure: A new treatment for military trauma, loss, and moral injury.* New York, NY: The Guilford Press.

Litz, B. T., Stein, N., Delaney, E., Lebowitz, L., Nash, W. P., Silva, C., & Maguen, S. (2009). Moral injury and moral repair in war veterans: A preliminary model and intervention strategy. *Clinical Psychology Review, 29*(8), 695–706. doi:10.1016/j.cpr.2009.07.003.

Manzella, C. & Papazoglou, K. (2014). Training police trainees about ways to manage trauma and loss. *International Journal of Mental Health Promotion, 16*(2), 103–116. doi:10.1080/14623730.2014.903609.

Marans, S. & Hahn, H. (2017). Enhancing police responses to children exposed to violence: A toolkit for law enforcement. *Office of Juvenile Justice and Delinquency Prevention, Office of Justice Programs, US Department of Justice.*

Marans, S., Smolover, D., & Hahn, H. (2012). Responding to child trauma: Theory, programs, and policy. In E. L. Girgorenko (Ed.), *Handbook of juvenile forensic psychology and psychiatry* (pp.453–466). New York: Springer.

Martin, A., Karanika-Murray, M., Biron, C., & Sanderson, K. (2014). The psychosocial work environment, employee mental health and organisational interventions: Improving research and practice by taking a multilevel approach. *Stress & Health, 32*(3), 201–215. doi:10.1002/smi.2593.

Maslach C., Jackson, S. E., & Leiter, M. P. (1996). *MBI: Maslach Burnout Inventory.* Sunnyvale, CA: CPP, Incorporated.

Mathieu, F. (2007). Running on empty: Compassion fatigue in health professionals. *Rehabilitation & Community Care Medicine, 4,* 1–7.

McFarlane, A. C. (2000). Posttraumatic stress disorder: A model of the longitudinal course and the role of risk factors. *Journal of Clinical Psychiatry, 61*(5), 15–23.

Memish, K., Martin, A., Bartlett, L., Dawkins, S., & Sanderson, K. (2017). Workplace mental health: An international review of guidelines. *Preventive Medicine, 101,* 213–222. doi:10.1016/j.ypmed.2017.03.017.

Miller, L. (2007). Police families: Stresses, syndromes, and solutions. *The American Journal of Family Therapy, 35*(1), 21–40. doi:10.1080/01926180600698541.

Mojtabai, R., Olfson, M., Sampson, N. A., Jin, R., Druss, B., Wang, P. S., Wells, K. B., Pincus, H. A., & Kessler, R. C. (2013). Barriers to mental health treatment: Results from the National Comorbidity Survey Replication. *Psychological Medicine, 41*(8), 1751–1761.doi:10.1017/S0033291710002291.

Nash, W. P., & Litz, B. T. (2013). Moral injury: A mechanism for war-related psychological trauma in military family members. *Clinical Child & Family Psychology Review, 16*(4), 365–375. doi:10.1007/s10567-013–0146-y.

Nazarov, A., Jetly, R., McNeely, H., Kiang, M., Lanius, R., & McKinnon, M. C. (2015). Role of morality in the experience of guilt and shame within the armed forces. *Acta Psychiatrica Scandinavica, 132*(1), 4–19. doi:10.1111/acps.12406.

Neff, K. D. (2003). Development and validation of a scale to measure self-compassion. *Self and Identity, 2,* 223–250. doi:10.1080/15298860309027.

Neff, K. D. (2012). The science of self-compassion. In C. Germer & R. Siegel (Eds.), *Compassion and wisdom in psychotherapy* (pp.79–92). Guilford Press.

Olson, A., & Wasilewski, M. (2016). *Suffering in silence: Mental health and stigma in policing.* Police One. https://www.policeone.com/police-products/human-resources/articles/218917006-Suffering-in-silence-Mental-health-and-stigma-in-policing/.

Papazoglou, K. (2017). The examination of different pathways leading towards police traumatization: Exploring the role of moral injury and personality in police compassion fatigue. *Dissertation Abstracts International: Section B: The Sciences and Engineering, 79(3-B).*

Papazoglou, K., Koskelainen, M., McQuerrey Tuttle, B., & Pitel, M. (2017). Examining the Role of Police Compassion Fatigue and Negative Personality Traits in Impeding the Promotion of Police Compassion Satisfaction: A Brief Report. *Journal of Law Enforcement, 6*(3), 1–14.

Park, M., Chang, E. R., & You, S. (2015). Protective role of coping flexibility in PTSD and depressive symptoms following trauma. *Personality and Individual Differences, 82,* 102–106. doi:10.1016/j.paid.2015.03.007.

Sayed, S., Iacoviello, B. M., & Charney, D. S. (2015). Risk factors for the development of. psychopathology following trauma. *Current Psychiatry Reports, 17*(8), 612. doi:10.1007/s11920-015–0612-y.

Shann, C., Martin, A., Chester, A., & Ruddock, S. (2019). Effectiveness and application of an online leadership intervention to promote mental health and reduce depression-related stigma in organizations. *Journal of Occupational Health Psychology, 24*(1), 20–35. doi:10.1037/ocp0000110.

Shay, J. (2014). Moral injury. *Psychoanalytic Psychology, 31*(2), 182–191. doi:10.1037/a0036090.

Simon, C. E., Pryce, J. G., Roff, L. L., & Klemmack, D. (2006). Secondary traumatic stress and.

oncology social work: Protecting compassion from fatigue and compromising the worker's worldview. *Journal of Psychosocial Oncology, 23*(4), 1–14. doi:10.1300/j077v23n04_01.

Slate, R. N., Johnson, W. W., & Colbert, S. S. (2007). Police stress: A structural model. *Journal of Police and Criminal Psychology, 22*(2), 102–112. doi:10.1007/s11896-007–9012-5.

Sprang, G., Clark, J. J., & Whitt-Woosley, A. (2007). Compassion fatigue, compassion satisfaction, and burnout: Factors impacting a professional's quality of life. *Journal of Loss and Trauma, 12*(3), 259–280. doi:10.1080/15325020701238093.

Sprang, G., Ford, J., Kerig, P., & Bride, B. (2019). Defining secondary traumatic stress and developing targeted assessments and interventions: Lessons learned from research and leading experts. *Traumatology, 25*(2), 72–81. doi:10.1037/trm0000180.

Stamm, B. H. (2010). The concise ProQOL Manual. Pocate, ID: ProQOL.org.

Stamm, B. H. (2002). Measuring compassion satisfaction as well as fatigue: Developmental history of the compassion satisfaction and fatigue test. In C. Figley (Ed.), *Treating Compassion Fatigue* (pp.107–119). Brunner-Routledge.

Standing Senate Committee on National Security and Defence (2015). *2015 Interim Report On The Operational Stress Injuries Of Canada's Veterans.* Retrieved from https://sencanada.ca/content/sen/Committee/412/secd/rep/rep17jun15-e.pdf.

Teasdale, J. D., Moore, R. G., Hayhurst H., Pope, M., Williams, S., & Segal, Z. V., (2002). Metacognitive awareness and prevention of relapse in depression: empirical evidence. *Journal of Consulting and Clinical Psychology, 70*:275. doi:10.1037/0022-006X.70.2.2775.

Violanti, J. M., Castellano, C., O'Rourke, J., & Paton, D. (2006). Proximity to the 9/11 terrorist attack and suicide ideation in police officers. *Traumatology, 12*(3), 248–254. doi:10.1177/1534765606296533.

Violanti, J. M., Mnatsakanova, A., Burchfiel, C. M., Hartley, T. A., & Andrew, M. E. (2012). Police suicide in small departments: A comparative analysis. *International Journal of Emergency Mental Health, 14*(3), 157–162.

Violanti, J. M., Owens, S. L., McCanlies, E., Fekedulegn, D., & Andrew, M. E. (2018). Law enforcement suicide: A review. *Policing: An International Journal, 42*(2), 141–164. doi:10.1108/PIJPSM-05–2017-0061.

Violanti, J. M., & Samuels, S. (2007). Trauma and police suicide ideation. In J. M. Violanti & S.

Samuels (Eds.), *Under the blue shadow: Clinical and behavioral perspectives on police suicide* (pp. 89–118). Charles C. Thomas.

Waters, J. A., & Ussery, W. (2007). Police stress: History, contributing factors, symptoms, and interventions. *Policing: An International Journal of Police Strategies & Management, 30*(2), 169–188. doi:10.1108/13639510710753199.

Weiss, D. S., Brunet, A., Best, S. R., Metzler, T. J., Liberman, A., Pole, N., Fagan, J. A., & Marmar, C. R. (2010). Frequency and severity approaches to indexing exposure to trauma: The Critical Incident History Questionnaire for police officers. *Journal of Traumatic Stress, 23*(6), 734–743. doi:10.1002/jts.20576.

Workman-Stark, A. L. (2017). Understanding police culture. In A. L., Workman-Stark (Ed.), *Inclusive Policing from the Inside Out* (pp. 19–35). Springer.

World Health Organisation. (2001). *World health report 2001. Mental health: New understanding, new hope*. Geneva, Switzerland.

World Health Organisation. (2008). *The global burden of disease: 2004 Update*. Geneva, Switzerland.

Wright, K., & Gudjonsson, G. H. (2007). The development of a scale for measuring offence-related feelings of shame and guilt. *Journal of Forensic Psychiatry & Psychology, 18*(3), 307–316. doi:10.1080/14789940701292810.

Wastell, C. A. (2002). Exposure to trauma: The long-term effects of suppressing emotional reactions. *The Journal of Nervous and Mental Disease, 190*(12), 839–845. doi:10.1097/01.NMD.0000042454.90472.4F.

Endnotes

1 Parts of this section 'compassion fatigue' have been published in C Russo, C. P. Aukhojee, B. M. Tuttle, O Johnson, M Davies, B Chopko & K Papazoglou as 'Compassion Fatigue and Burnout' in K Papazoglou & D. M. Blumberg (eds), *Power: Police Officers Wellness, Ethics, & Resilience*, Elsevier-Academic Press, San Diego 2019, pp. 97–115.

2 Parts of this section on moral injury have been published in K. Papazoglou & D. M. Blumberg (eds), *Power: Police Officers Wellness, Ethics, & Resilience*, pp. 117–128.

10 Protecting those safeguarding our community

John Bale

The emergency services and national security sectors protect and care for our community. In carrying out their duties there is a high risk they will experience trauma that negatively impacts their lives. While this statement might seem obvious, the conversation about the mental health of the emergency services and national security community has emerged more slowly than it has within similar vocations, the most obvious parallel being the veteran community. Veterans, like emergency services and national security personnel—to whom we refer as 'first responders'—face real risks to their mental wellbeing simply by doing their job. The disparity in awareness of the impacts of these jobs is stark. This is, in part, due to the impact of the Iraq and Afghanistan conflicts: these brutal asymmetric wars came at a high cost of lives lost and limbs injured, and the enduring nature of these wars also highlighted the mental health impacts in a way unseen in previous conflicts. Assessing the impacts of generations of veterans deploying and returning home has built significant quantitative and qualitative data to show us the impacts of these conflicts. Without this catalyst of war, the first responder community has not, until very recently, built this same rich data set.

The lack of close attention is beginning to change, led by initiatives such as Beyond Blue's 2018 ground-breaking research, 'Answering the Call', the first national survey of the mental health and wellbeing of Australian police and emergency services personnel. More than 21,000 people took part in this survey, providing a detailed and accurate picture of mental health issues affecting these first responders. The research shows that one in two emergency services personnel will experience a traumatic event that deeply affects them during the course of their work. One in three emergency services personnel will experience high or very high psychological distress in their lifetime.[1] This is more than twice the rate of the general Australian adult population (Australian Bureau of Statistics (ABS), 2015) and substantially higher than that of the Australian Defence Force.

The longer an individual serves their community in the emergency services, the higher chance they have of being impacted by a mental health injury. Employees who had worked more than 10 years were almost twice as likely to experience psychological distress and were six times more likely to experience symptoms of post-traumatic stress disorder (PTSD).[2] These statistics extend to the suicide health crisis. Suicidal thoughts are twice as common in emergency services employees and volunteers than in adults in the general population (ABS, 2016), and first responders are over three times more likely to have a suicide plan (ABS, 2016).

The complexities and traumas facing first responders are not isolated to Australia. These effects are felt worldwide. The lessons of other developed nations are applicable in our understanding of how to best address the mental health of our first responders. International research on the impacts of the roles and work of first responders is emerging, led by considerable research in the United States, Britain and Canada. This is important as the work undertaken by first responders is becoming increasingly complex and larger in scale. The 2019–20 'Black Summer' fires and the disruption caused by COVID-19 highlight these impacts.

Kings College London, Open Universities, and the Royal Foundation have released a comprehensive study that is similar in scope to Beyond Blue's 'Answering the Call'. Titled 'Assessing the mental health and wellbeing of the emergency responder community in the United Kingdom',[3] indicates that:

- Emergency Responders (ERs) experience specific occupational stressors associated with poor mental health and wellbeing outcomes. On average, the evidence indicated that ERs may experience more mental health problems, such as depression, anxiety.[4]
- In both the systematic review and stakeholder interviews, organisational stressors (such as excessive workloads and lack of senior

support) were found to negatively impact ERs' mental health and wellbeing, more than critical incident stressors (such as potentially traumatic accident scenes).[5]

· Organisational support and good leadership were associated with improved wellbeing, morale and retention, according to ER studies.[6]

These findings are similar to those within the work completed by Beyond Blue, the findings of the Senate Inquiry, 'The People Behind 000,' the Independent Mental Health Review conducted on Victoria Police (published 2016), and the Australian National Audit Office (ANAO) report conducted on the mental health programs of the Australian Federal Police (AFP) in 2017.

While the vocational mental health focus has been on veterans and their families, it is clear that in doing their job, our emergency services personnel also run an immense risk to their mental health. While some lessons in how to mitigate these risks can be found from the data and measures undertaken by the veteran community, the emergency services community is, in numerous ways, a different cohort who require a specialised approach.

Fortem exists to provide this specialised approach for the first responder community.

Filling the gap for families
The families of emergency services personnel have tended to be overlooked in research and workplace programs. Families are a key part of many first responders' daily lives. Ten per cent of rural volunteers reported that balancing brigade commitments and family life was very difficult, especially for those with young children.[7] Although family members are not directly exposed to the traumas that a loved one faces as a first responder, they are still significantly impacted by this trauma. Research conducted into the impacts of war-related trauma highlights that trauma is not just experienced by veterans, it also extends to their children and partners, who are negatively affected by the trauma as they live with, and care for, the veteran.[8] Trauma within a family unit can ripple through family relationships and impede optimal family functioning, with partners of veterans with PTSD[9] reporting inner feelings of loneliness, and the children of veterans with war-related PTSD having higher levels of behavioural problems.[10]

Despite the lack of research into first responder families, it is expected that many of the issues identified in veteran families are mirrored in first responder families. Bessel van der Kolk described how children are impacted by a parent's PTSD:

> Children in such families invariably grow up with distorted ideas about their roles in family conflicts: they are likely to blame themselves and carry around a core of self-hatred that is difficult to undo later in life. These children often develop difficulties in emotional involvement with others; their object relations frequently are characterised by withdrawal and caution lest the wounds of emotional betrayal once again be opened, or by intense involvements and repeated disappointments as nobody is found who can compensate for the sense of loss and betrayal they have carried since childhood.[11]

The lack of family-based research or programs does not seem restricted to the Australian emergency services community. In 2018–19, I visited the United States, the United Kingdom and Canada and spoke with members of numerous law enforcement and emergency services organisations, some of which appear in this book. In Britain there was only one study fitting the search criteria in the emergency responder (ER) field,[12] which identified pressures on ER spouses and children. These pressures include the impact of shift work, lone parenting, concerns for ER safety and ER work stress/trauma that negatively affected spouses' and children's psychological wellbeing and family functioning.[13] Many families require mental health support during times of significant stress and trauma. Currently, there are no known independent programs that provide this mental health support to these families, running the risk of the family unit taking on the vicarious, secondary and sometimes transgenerational trauma associated with the first responder's role.

Fortem is unique in our approach to support not only first responders, but also their family members, in order to help families create stronger connections, and build greater mental health and resilience.

Providing stronger support for volunteers
Volunteer first responders are consistently called upon to participate in complex and traumatising work, often for extended periods. For example, volunteers were the largest group of first responders involved in fighting the

Black Summer fires of 2019–20. These volunteer roles are highly dangerous and stressful,[14] resulting[15] in general mental health concerns, including depression,[16] and traumatic stress symptoms as well as an increased risk to psychiatric morbidity following large scale traumatic incidents. Despite the general mental health issues faced by volunteer firefighters and first responders in general, there are limited studies undertaken on the impacts of post-traumatic stress on firefighters after large scale national disasters. These same volunteers, then, have limited access to the necessary support services for mental health problems.[17]

The limited research does show that volunteer first responders are at an increased risk of trauma-related mental health problems,[18] and for those that attend more trauma related incidents the risk of probable PTSD was significantly higher.[19] Milligan-Saville found that:

> This psychiatric vulnerability may be attributed to the lack of pre-employment psychological screening (Guo et al., 2004); increased work-family conflict due to the extra demands of the volunteer role (Cowlishaw et al., 2008); minimal training on mental health and critical incidents (Brazil, 2017) and greater structural barriers to mental health care (Stanley et al., 2017), although many of these hypotheses have not been empirically tested.

A key recommendation of the Senate inquiry, conducted by the Education and Employment References Committee, 'The people behind 000: mental health of our first responders', is that mental health support services be extended to all first responder volunteers.[20] Currently the level of mental health services provided to volunteer first responder organisations is inconsistent with that offered to their paid colleagues. In the Senate inquiry, the Royal Australian and New Zealand College of Psychiatrists' (RANZCP) submission highlighted that volunteer first responders, and especially those that come from rural and regional areas, are vulnerable for specific reasons:

> A 2015 study found that rural and regional ambulance workers face unique issues, including treating personally known patients, working alone and long response times. This study also found that rural and regional ambulance personnel experience high levels of fatigue and emotional trauma at work while an earlier study reported increased

levels of fatigue and depression, anxiety and stress, and poor quality sleep. Rural and remote communities also have a widely acknowledged disadvantage when it comes to accessing mental health services, due to geographical barriers, maldistribution of medical professionals and unique circumstances surrounding stigma in such communities. In particular, access to specialists, such as psychiatrists, may be limited.[21]

Resourcing, distance, a predominately rural and regional volunteer force and a workforce that is difficult to build greater data on, due to their volunteer nature, has resulted in volunteers having less than ideal mental health support services. Volunteer first responder families are also clearly impacted by the trauma that their loved ones experience. Again, there is little research and limited programs provided for this cohort.

The support of first responder families, and especially those of volunteers in regional and rural areas, is a key focus of Fortem's programs.

Increasing mental health literacy
Mental health literacy within the first responder community is anecdotally poor. Stigma, fear, limited understanding of signs and symptoms of poor mental health, and a lack of trust for the Employee Assistance Program (EAP) or organisational health programs appear prevalent. Mental health literacy programs are not systemic within most jurisdictions. Victoria Police, after completing an internal assessment of their mental health programs, recognised the limited focus on mental health literacy within their organisation,[22] highlighting the need for access to such programs and support services. Building an understanding of what good mental health looks like, the drivers to poor mental health and the risks that can impact mental health are important not only for the individual first responder, but also for their interactions with the public. First responders are seeing more and more cases where mental health injuries have resulted in their call-out, making an understanding of mental health critical in everyday situations.

The most relevant barrier to care that currently exists within emergency services organisations is mental health stigma, and mental health literacy is a critical element in combating this. It is difficult to de-stigmatise mental health injuries or intervention without everyone understanding the drivers that make up good mental health.

Fortem provides psychological care programs that build the mental health literacy of first responders and their families, encouraging them to undertake preventative lifestyle factors and seek help as needed.

Removing the stigma barrier

Stigma is a term that refers to various types of social, cultural and personal factors affecting access to mental health care. It is defined as a 'negative and erroneous attitude about a person, a prejudice, or negative stereotype.'[23] Stigma is one of the main reasons people do not seek mental health care. Social cognitive processes motivate people to avoid the label of mental illness that results when people are associated with mental health care.[24] Katy Kamkar and Konstantinos Papazoglou claim that stigma is the largest barrier to help seeking (Lasalvia, 2013) and that continuous effort and creative strategies need to be delivered for stigma reduction. Stigma is a barrier to effective care. It is unique in this respect. While the barriers that exist for physical healthcare, such as a lack of trained health care staff or the provision of sick leave to attend sessions, are physical impediments to recovery, the same cannot be said of stigma. In first responder agencies, stigma represents an invisible barrier holding individuals back from good quality clinical support.

Corrigan has identified two distinct types of stigma surrounding mental health injuries. The first is public stigma, which he defines as 'what a naive public does to the stigmatised group when they endorse the prejudice about said group'. The public stigma attached to having a mental illness and receiving a psychiatric diagnosis has been the subject of extensive study in both military and civilian contexts.[25] Those publicly labelled as mentally ill are harmed in several ways. Stereotypes, prejudice and discrimination can prevent these people from achieving important life goals. Evidence suggests that public identification of someone as 'mentally ill' can cause significant harm. Research has shown that people with concealable stigmas (people who are gay, of minority faith-based communities, or with mental illness) decide to avoid this harm by hiding their condition.[26] Alternatively, they may opt to avoid the stigma altogether by denying their group status and by not seeking assistance from those institutions that will signal their condition (mental health care, for example). This kind of label avoidance is perhaps the most common way in which stigma impedes care-seeking and is the most relevant to institutional settings such as first responder agencies.

The second type of stigma identified in mental health injuries is self-stigma, which Corrigan refers to as 'what members of a stigmatised group may do to themselves if they internalise the public stigma'.[27]

> I perceived myself, quite accurately unfortunately, as having a serious mental illness and therefore as having been relegated to what I called 'the social garbage heap' ... I tortured myself with the persisted persistent and repetitive thought that people I would encounter, even total strangers, did not like me and wished that mentally ill people like me did not exist.
>
> Thus, I would do things such as standing away from others at bus stops and hiding and cringing in the far corners of subway cars. Thinking of myself as garbage, I would even leave the sidewalk in what I thought of as exhibiting the proper deference to those above me in social class. The latter group, of course, included all other human beings.[28]

Narratives such as this indicate that self-prejudice leads to negative emotional reactions; prominent among these is low self-esteem and low self-efficacy.[29]

The stigma of mental health injuries affects the family as well as the individual and, in many instances, the family of someone experiencing a mental health injury will hide the condition and fail to seek support. In other situations it may be family members who, under extraordinary pressure, make the decision to seek care and support for the affected individual, sometimes without that person's knowledge. In both scenarios a program aimed at educating and supporting the families of those with mental health injuries is a logical and simple option to combat stigma and help families become more cohesive.

At Fortem, we advocate within first responder agencies and educate the public about the challenges for first responders and their families, in order to normalise mental health challenges and reduce the stigma that exists.

Strengthening the ability of first responders to stay at work

Job security is vital to first responders, especially those who are in paid employment. Being a first responder is key to the perceived self-worth of many who serve, and termination of employment is a dramatic and often confronting experience that first responders will do almost anything to avoid.

The fear of being discharged due to the disclosure of a mental health injury is currently a significant barrier to care. Promises made by the senior leadership of first responder agencies do little to reassure the lower ranks who are among those most affected by mental health injuries. The most effective way to allay fears over job security for those who seek treatment for mental health injuries is to highlight positive experiences from currently serving first responders who have been rehabilitated and subsequently enjoy successful careers. These first responders' stories, highlighting a successful return to their career, present a highly effective means of reassuring those with mental health injuries that they can, particularly with early intervention, be rehabilitated rather than discharged from their role.

This message can be useful in reinforcing the need for early intervention, signalling the fact that the sooner individual sufferers seek help, the greater the chance of their recovery, and the less likely they are to face discharge. This will ultimately reduce the burden of mental health injuries on the individual, their family, the first responder agency, and the wider community.

Security clearances are also important to many who work within the AFP and Australian Border Force. The loss or removal of a security clearance can severely affect an individual's ability to operate efficiently. The removal of a security clearance due to mental health concerns can also have a dramatic effect on the individual's sense of worth and purpose. Although security clearances are not immediately removed on the disclosure of mental health injuries, a reading of the '2020 Australian Government Personnel Security Adjudicative Guidelines' would raise concerns for anyone considering treatment:

> Behaviour that casts doubt on a clearance subject's judgement, reliability, or trustworthiness that is not covered under any other guideline, including but not limited to emotionally unstable, irresponsible, dysfunctional, violent, paranoid, or bizarre behaviour.[30]

This requirement exists despite the guidelines being recently changed to include the statement that: 'No negative inference concerning the standards in these guidelines may be raised solely based on seeking mental health counselling.'[31] Remaining in purposeful employment is a major factor in the good mental health of first responders and, therefore, their families.

Fortem is working towards programs that help first responders maintain employment, whether that is in a first responder agency or transitioning to other work.

Improving workplace and economic costs

Besides the personal and cultural impacts of being mentally injured by these vocations, it is important to consider the workplace and economic impacts that this can have on each organisation. From the publicly available data provided through agencies' annual reports, the combined workers compensation premiums for state-based emergency services organisations, AFP and Australian Border Force is well over a combined $650 million.

Workers compensation premiums are provided for all injuries that may befall an organisation's workforce. While physical injuries still dominate in most organisations, mental health injuries are growing in their weighting. Ambulance Victoria reports that mental health claims make up 8 per cent of workers compensation claims but account for 24 per cent of the cost.[32] The 2019 New South Wales Police Annual Report shows that mental health claims are the third most frequent type of workers compensation claim (following body stress and being hit by moving objects), with 2.6 claims per 100 full-time equivalent (FTE) employees.[33] In Victoria Police, mental health related injuries make up 28 per cent of the WorkCover claims, yet account for 70 per cent of total claim cost.[34] With mental health injury claims continuing to increase, agencies' premiums will continue to rise. Despite the AFP having approximately 6,695 staff and the Department of Defence having nearly 60,000 uniformed members, the AFP ComCare bill is almost double that of Defence.

Mental health injuries obviously have a significant impact on the dynamics of a workforce. While physical injuries seem to have a high rate of return to work—93 per cent in Victoria Police—psychological injuries have a much lower rate: 64 per cent for Victoria Police in the same period.[35] These premiums are unsustainable. As mental health injuries continue to become a larger proportion of workers compensation claims, more investment needs to be considered to drive down the rate of mental health injury.

Fortem highlights the importance of families and other protective factors to improve these economic outcomes.

Creating social connection

Connection is one of the most important elements of the preventative factors that can be practised by both first responder personnel and their families. Social connection refers to several inter-related factors denoting the support a person receives from their social networks, and this can play a protective role in maintaining wellbeing in the face of repeated exposure to severe stressors.

Studies show that social connection is a building block for good mental health. The recent senate inquiry indicates that police, in particular, struggle with isolation from their community once they retire or are no longer operational.[36] A study by Beyond Blue shows that those with limited social connectedness are more likely to have probable PTSD.[37] This is supported by international research, which highlights a robust body of evidence showing that a lack of social support is one of the strongest predictors of PTSD after exposure to a traumatic event.[38] Resilience to repeated traumatic exposure is bolstered by protective psychosocial factors relating to social connectedness and community involvement.

Trauma is not always a negative experience. It can and does lead to post-traumatic growth. Social connection plays a role in this happening. The term 'post-traumatic growth' refers to positive psychological change experienced because of the struggle with highly challenging life circumstances, and it is only possible with strong social support. People who had strong social support were more likely to undergo positive psychological changes or personal development after experiencing trauma.[39] The protective effect of social relationships seems to extend not only to general mental health but also to mortality risk. Studies have predicted the risk for mortality, irrespective of causes of death and initial health status, at a rate comparable with well-established mortality risk factors, such as smoking, alcohol consumption and lack of physical exercise.[40] Social connectedness plays an important role in predicting mortality risk and suggests that individuals with strong social relationships are likely to remain alive longer than their counterparts with poor social connection.

There is a consistent finding that positive mental health and wellbeing are tied to strong social connectedness. The core factors underpinning this relationship centre largely on social support, community engagement, family and relationship cohesion, and self-perceived levels of loneliness. First responders would benefit throughout their careers if there was a stronger focus on developing better social connection programs.

Although all of Fortem's programs have social connection as a key focus, our wellbeing activities are especially geared towards getting people to connect and build networks that can make them and their family more resilient.

External program alternatives

Organisations that place people into potentially traumatic instances, such as emergency services, national security agencies and defence forces, as well as trauma nurses and doctors, recognise that, as part of their duty of care, they need to provide internal services that can support the individual's mental health and wellbeing. The availability and effectiveness of these services is inconsistent and in various stages of maturity. Often there are no systemic arrangements to evaluate support service effectiveness on a continuing basis. The previously outlined barriers to accessing support and assistance—such as stigma and concerns for job security—continue to reduce the potential impact of these services.

Many mental health programs that are provided by agencies do not have a framework to evaluate their effectiveness and management arrangements. Often there are limitations towards engagement and feedback from staff on the usefulness of these programs as well as which programs are both effective and popular. While logic would dictate that the mental health programs provided by these organisations are predominantly focused on the trauma of the roles undertaken by first responders, the evidence highlights that organisational health actually supports a range of personal issues that have emerged through the stress of the role, cultural issues at work or home-based stressors. Forty-six per cent of counselling referrals indicate a work-related matter as the primary reason, which includes exposure to trauma. The remaining 54 per cent present with 'personal' issues.[41]

This dimension is a vital aspect of these internal programs because, as much as work trauma can impact the family of a first responder, family issues can also impact the workplace performance of the first responder. There are limited Australian studies on the impact of home life on the performance of first responders. Anecdotally, however, organisational mental health programs highlight that people experiencing serious home issues, such as the dissolving of a long-term relationship or a significant illness or injury, are more likely to seek internal resources than those of EAPs. My suspicion is that more first responders in these situation are more likely to seek outside help.

Families, too, often feel that they cannot access internal support services, or are discouraged to do so by their first responder partner, for a fear of connecting their issue with their partner's employer. As such, mental health issues often stay under the surface in organisations as families and individuals will not use the services that they are offered, regardless of their effectiveness.

There are EAP structures in place. Originally established to support people with alcohol issues, EAPs have grown to act as a catch-all for businesses to support individuals through issues internal to the organisation, such as workplace conflict and low-level job-related stressors. EAPs also support personal issues that might impact a person's performance in the workplace, such as the loss of a loved one, alcohol or drug issues, the loss of a relationship or deterioration in the home environment.[42] While EAP services are general in nature and designed to give short term support, they also often suffer from a poor engagement rate. In the 'Mental Health in the Australian Federal Police'

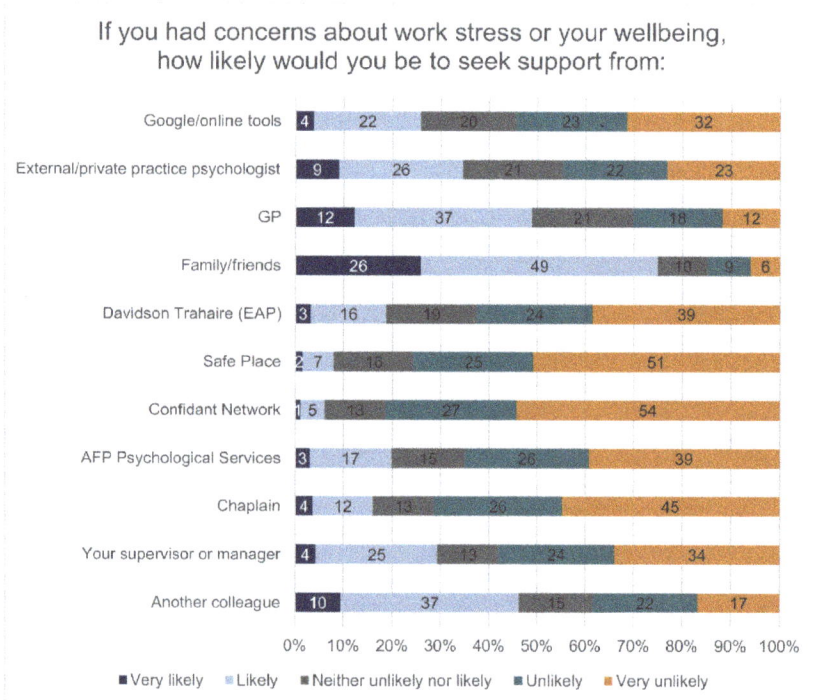

If you had concerns about work stress or your wellbeing, how likely would you be to seek support from:

	Very likely	Likely	Neither unlikely nor likely	Unlikely	Very unlikely
Google/online tools	4	22	20	23	32
External/private practice psychologist	9	26	21	22	23
GP	12	37	21	18	12
Family/friends	26	49	10	9	6
Davidson Trahaire (EAP)	3	16	10	24	39
Safe Place	2	7	16	25	51
Confidant Network	1	5	13	27	54
AFP Psychological Services	3	17	15	26	39
Chaplain	4	12	13	26	45
Your supervisor or manager	4	25	13	24	34
Another colleague	10	37	15	22	17

Support seeking preferences of sworn respondents (n=1164)

Chart 1

Inquiry completed by Phoenix Australia in 2017–18,[43] only 3 per cent of their sworn workforce were 'highly likely' to utilise the EAP support services if they had concerns about stress or wellbeing; a further 16 per cent were 'likely' while 63 per cent were either 'unlikely' or 'highly unlikely'. Instead, seeking support from within the family unit was by far the most likely place to turn, with 75 per cent saying they were either 'highly likely' or 'likely' to ask family and friends for help, and only 15 per cent highlighting they were 'unlikely' or 'highly unlikely' to turn to their loved ones.[44] (See Chart 1).

Due to their general nature, EAP services also find it difficult to address the cultural needs of first responder agencies. This issue can result in first responders not building a rapport with their EAP, and the EAP receiving a bad reputation.[45]

It is not only members of the first responder organisation that have access to the EAP services: such services are usually available to families. Some 28 per cent of people using the AFP's EAP service are family members. While the number of family members using the service is reported for billing purposes, the range of matters discussed is not reported to the AFP.[46]

In its review of AFP mental health programs, Phoenix Australia recommended that the AFP:

> Undertake a review of the EAP contract, including the suitability of the current EAP, to ensure that individuals providing services to AFP staff are appropriately qualified (preferably as clinical psychologists), understand the work of the AFP (cultural competence) and provide consistency in service provision (i.e., individuals see the same counsellor for each of their up-to-six sessions).[47]

Fortem's offering is in part designed to fill the gaps that EAPs were neither established to provide nor in many instances able to. Specifically, Fortem can support the longer-term wellbeing of the individual outside of the work environment, while being a specialist in the stressors, traumas and cultures of emergency services and national security organisations. Regardless of the attempts of organisations to remove or reduce stigma, often people simply do not want to express their emotions or setbacks, whether caused by the job or family or personal pressures, in a workplace setting. Fortem offers an important external alternative to the already established internal support services provided by first responder organisations.

Designing programs for families

Fortem Australia's mission is to improve and protect the health and wellbeing of the people who keep our communities safe. We are a not-for-profit organisation that supports the mental fitness and wellbeing of first responder families. Every day, more than 300,000 first responders keep our communities safe. They are backed up by their families: partners, children and parents. All of them hold vital, and challenging, roles. We help them to be well, and stay well, through mental fitness and wellbeing activities and support services.

- We support first responder families to improve and protect their mental fitness.
- We connect families together to strengthen family bonds.
- We activate community and individual awareness and education.
- We collaborate with organisations to foster a collective effort to improve wellbeing.

Fortem provides evidence-based, comprehensive, and integrated wellbeing support designed to complement the programs already in place within first responder agencies. We have identified that there is no federal, state or territory connective body for the sharing of first responder mental health and wellbeing programs. This was also established as a point by the report, 'The people behind 000: mental health of our first responders.'[48] Whereas the advice of that committee was for the Commonwealth to build a co-designed approach with the various governments, Fortem is focusing on the development of inter-agency leadership forums to build better understanding of the programs that currently exist within each of these jurisdictions, and to support collaboration and collective de-stigmatisation efforts.

Fortem is also focused on the ability for agencies and individuals to have access to the wide range of current health and wellbeing programs offered at a federal, state and territory level. Often states do not build the collective knowledge around services that are available, simply through a lack of understanding about what current programs are available. Fortem, while ensuring eligible members have a greater understanding of the services their organisations already provide, offers external alternatives to encourage care-seeking for first responder families (including the serving member).[49]

Prevention is better than a cure

Many of the services currently available are reactive to crisis. They do not help build protective and preventative barriers. While recovery from any mental health injury is possible, the recovery process for both the individual and their family is physically, emotionally, and often financially burdensome. We believe in a positive psychology framework: that it is beneficial to protect against and prevent mental health injuries.

Primary prevention and protective factors are key to Fortem's support of first responder families. Katy Kamkar and Konstantinos Papazoglou explain the difference between primary, secondary and tertiary prevention:

> Primary prevention is aimed towards reducing the onset or likelihood of an illness. It generally involves building resiliency through a two-step process: reducing risk factors and building protective factors. Any proactive education and mental health promotion can fall within the primary prevention care (e.g., online resiliency training). Secondary prevention involves any interventions aimed at identifying and address-ing health problems at an early stage (e.g., screening tests). Tertiary prevention care involves evidence-based treatment and interventions, and disability management (e.g., evidence-based cognitive behavioural treatment with work interventions) aimed at reducing disability and improving overall functioning and return to work.[50]

Fortem is focused on giving first responder families easy access to the protective factors that will build their resilience. Protective factors are uni-versally applicable for any person or family. However, their implementation is vital for first responder families as their resilience will be tested through the almost guaranteed traumatisation of their first responder. As Kamkar and Papazoglou have stressed:

> Coping flexibility is the ability to utilise flexibility and different coping strategies in a particular situation (Bonanno, Pat-Horenczyk, & Noll, 2011) and has been found to be associated with lower levels of posttrau-matic stress and depressive symptoms after controlling for co-morbid

symptoms, age and time since the traumatic event (Park, Chang, & You, 2015).

The protective factors that Fortem works with families to establish in their daily lives are:

- strong support networks, such as family, friends and community;
- positive sense of identity;
- being physically healthy and taking care of yourself through lifestyle factors such as exercising, eating well and reducing stress where possible;
- good coping and problem-solving skills;
- optimism and a belief that life has meaning and hope;
- a positive attitude to support seeking; and
- access to support services, including mental health support that understands you.

While our programs support the continuum of mental health and wellbeing, our focus is on ensuring first responder families can thrive through the adversity of their roles. To build successful programs and ensure that we deliver outcomes that are linked to primary prevention evidence, Fortem works within a framework that is built around the Five Ways to Wellbeing. This framework incorporates a series of pillars.

Connect

Connection is based on developing close relationships and socialising with friends, family and others, as well as broadening social and support networks and a range of relationships in the wider community. Connection underpins many of Fortem's activities—such as family weekends, team building activities and trivia nights—because the benefits are wide-ranging and integral to first responder families' wellbeing, and social integration and cohesion.

Be active

Regular physical activity is a cornerstone of good mental health. It prevents and reduces symptoms of depression, anxiety and stress. It helps improve sleep quality, detracts from negative thoughts, and improves confidence and resilience. We offer active programs, such as surfing, walking groups and cycling to encourage physical activity for improved health and wellbeing.

Be aware

Research shows that being mindful—that is, focusing on the present—can reduce stress, increase resilience, and build self-awareness that can lead to greater mental health literacy. We include mindfulness into activities such as yoga, creative arts, and courses in mindfulness practices.

Learn

Learning new skills helps to improve thinking skills and increase the ability to cope with stress, as well as boosting confidence, enabling a connection with others and finding purpose. We offer a range of varied skills to learn, including music lessons, language classes and practical skills.

Give

Studies show that acts of kindness are linked to increased feelings of wellbeing and can also create a sense of belonging while reducing isolation. Kindness to others can also help keep things in perspective. Fortem helps participants to give back through volunteering and mentoring opportunities, as well as encouraging the wider community to show gratitude through our annual 'Thank a First Responder Day'.

These five pillars underpin our programs within the following categories:

- *Wellbeing programs*: activities to support connection and wellbeing to ensure those with (developing/existing) mental health concerns and their families do not become further isolated, while also building resilience and health/help seeking behaviours for all.
- *Case Management and community engagement*: Fortem case managers bridge the gap between psychology appointments and support activities to ensure continuity of care, welfare needs are met, on referrals to external and community organisations and ongoing trauma support, an important element on the road to recovery.
- *Mental fitness support*: Our psychological services are delivered in person and via telehealth (phone and online) for first responder families. Our team of psychologists deliver a centralised intake, assessing and triaging needs, as well as undertaking group programs that educate first responder families in mental fitness. This is a trusted service which is external to the workplace, and which works to increase mental health literacy.

These activities are designed and implemented following the health promotion program planning cycle.

Step 1: Identify need: This may be informed by a range of sources such as consultation with the community, feedback from Community Engagement Coordinators or Care Coordinators, feedback from participants, literature reviews, research articles and accepted/current evidence base.

Step 2: Program planning: This includes ensuring a selected activity aligns with the Five Ways to Wellbeing framework and has a suitable evidence-base for use, and also takes into consideration: target audience (e.g. families, individuals, couples); whether it is open to all agencies or only one (preference is that most activities are open to members from all agencies; what is the goal of the activity (i.e. what is the desired outcome?); and, evaluation plan.

Step 3: Implementation of activity and monitoring: Activity is implemented, participation is monitored, if needed participants are referred to other services.

Step 4: Evaluation: All activities are evaluated, and the tools and metrics used for this are regularly updated based on the expected outcomes and uptake. All activity evaluation plans include measures of uptake, satisfaction, process, impact and outcome.

From 'Surf Therapy' programs to coffee catch-ups, yoga classes to creative writing workshops, these programs and activities have a range of purposes

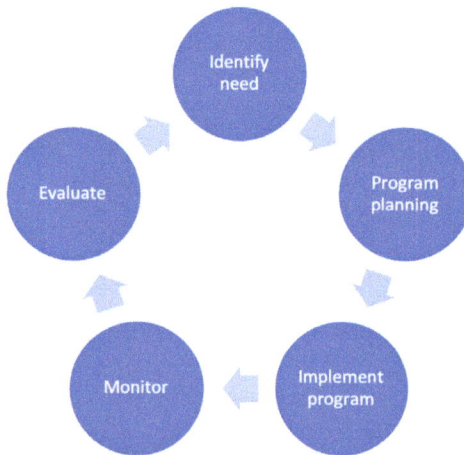

Fig 1: Health promotion program planning cycle

and benefits to meet the various needs of the first responder families Fortem supports. In-house programming also has the flexibility to tailor to the needs of the presenting cohort and adapt to a changing landscape of ill-health, respite support, and focused psycho-education. Importantly, these roles take place within the community, meaning the money goes straight back into regional communities, and especially those suffering from the Black Summer fires and the continuing impacts of COVID-19.

'Success' and future plans

Fortem has proven success in the delivery of high-quality programs. Since our establishment in October 2019, Fortem has engaged with over 1,000 first responder and national security participants and delivered weekly in-person activities (prior to COVID-19) and over 20 virtual events to families across Australia, with more scheduled. We have also hosted three de-stigmatisation events broadcast through all national security agencies, with an audience of over 10,000 people. Fortem has initiated and is facilitating a national day of appreciation for first responders, 'Thank a First Responder Day' on 2 June 2020, in conjunction with first responder organisations nationally and with public support from a range of high-profile politicians and celebrities. Fortem is also coordinating the upcoming inaugural Leadership and Mental Health Summit for figureheads of national and state first responder agencies, in addition to initiating connection between service support organisations to enhance the awareness, quality and coordination of offerings for the first responder community.

Fortem has grown rapidly since launching. Within the next five years, we will increase the scale of our proven services across all of Australia's states and territories. Our aim is to ensure that all first responder families are supported by our wellbeing programs, case management and community engagement services, and mental fitness support. These programs are already being delivered across much of the east coast of Australia and will extend to include all states and territories, and all paid and volunteer organisations. The extension of these services will especially focus on regional and rural areas in which community-based support services are typically low. Fortem will help build broader capacity to deliver high quality evidence-based programs in each location we establish our services.

Like the delivery of its current programs, Fortem will work with each of the state and territory first responder agencies, the AFP and Australian Border Force to ensure that our programs continue to complement the services they provide internally and improve health seeking behaviours. Our continued focus on first responder families and the individual first responder as part of the family unit will allow for a strong uptake of protective health strategies universally (Australia-wide) but also locally (geographic and organisational considerations). We will employ people that are connected to their community, in order to build trust and accountability.

Transition support

One of the key recommendations from the recent Beyond Blue research was transition support for those transitioning out of service. In addition to the programs that have been outlined in this chapter and their extension to all states and territories, Fortem is preparing to pilot a transition support service to first responder families. In this, we will take a national approach to ensuring first responders get the support they deserve when leaving, either voluntarily or through medical requirements for their organisation, and start a job outside of their first responder role.

The transition from being an active first responder can be a difficult one for both the transitioning person, their families and those in the team who remain on active duty. The separation is particularly difficult for those medically transitioning from service, and their teams, because of the often unexpected nature of the transition. The transition process for first responders is anecdotally not always a smooth one, which results in members staying in roles longer than they should. This has a negative impact on the first responder who is unable to proceed to their next career in a timely manner and can adversely affect the morale of the remaining team members.

Some first responders on transition have reported extended social isolation. By creating a culture in which staff are confident around the transition process, and by removing concern around transition, Fortem will assist first responder agencies in creating a workplace that is more task-focussed while personnel continue to serve without fear of what is ahead in their career, and put protective factors in place for the transitioning member to ensure a timely transition. Having a transition program linked with existing, independent, social connection programs creates links to those who have already had a successful and pleasant transition process. It allows current serving members who have close relationships with those who are transitioning to see that transitioning members are treated with respect, and develops a level of trust.

Modelled on a national veterans' employment program, Fortem has been working to ensure that there have been many adjustments and tweaks made to ensure this program works for the first responder cohort. The pilot will focus on selected policing jurisdictions. If this pilot is successful, Fortem then intends to deliver transition support to all state and territory first responder agencies. This support would include everyone who is transitioning Australia-wide, not just those who are leaving on medical grounds. First responder families deserve gainful employment after their service ends. They have all given a lot to protect and care for their community, while building many transferable skills.

Part of this transition program will be to build the understanding that private industry has of the diverse skills that first responders are trained with and the ways in which these skills are transferable into the private sector. Taking former first responders into a business should be a competitive advantage, and Fortem will work with the business community to ensure these messages resound within both boardrooms and human resources departments. Employment within the current economic climate will be especially difficult for any first responder moving out of their organisation. The support that Fortem will provide—including coaching, mentoring and linking first responders to private industries that can still employ new hires—will be critical. Without this focus, there is a risk that first responders, who have been often at the front line of our most pressing emergencies, including COVID-19, will be disadvantaged. We intend to use our specialised focus on first responders to ensure that transitioning to other meaningful employment is a positive experience.

Mental health support and preventative care

The concept of mental health within our society often brings negative connotations. When commenting on a person's mental health, we focus on the issues they face. Saying 'mental health' does not lead us to question how a person is building their resilience or draw our attention to protective mental health factors.

This is a complex issue for Fortem. While delivering a range of programs that focus on family protective factors, we will also provide clinical services to those who have suffered PTSD from their work-related traumas. To support this wide-ranging group, we recognise that mental health is a spectrum. Like physical health, we focus on the development of powerful networks, healthy techniques and regular training to ensure that good mental health can be maintained. To combat the obvious stigma that does, and perhaps always will, exist around the term mental health, Fortem stresses the positive and inclusive programs we offer. When a first responder family is socially connected and linked to their community, they will be in a much better position to be resilient in dealing with their jobs. With a newfound understanding of mental health literacy, first responder families will also be able to detect or discern the symptoms of mental health deterioration and be able to access the right help.

Respecting this spectrum, we will invest heavily in building more resilient families through easily accessible services designed to improve protective factors. When an individual or family needs further support, Fortem will direct them to our in-house clinical services. We believe this will increase trust in clinical services and assist people in feeling able to access these supports earlier. Building an organisation that is both for everyone, and also accessed for its mental health services, is a complex balancing act. Our approach with families and preventative and protective factors will be key to ensuring that both Fortem and the concepts of mental fitness do not become stigmatised. It will take considerable effort to ensure we can 'message' what Fortem is going to achieve, but also to engage with the wider public to present a more nuanced appraisal of the issues facing first responder families.

In earlier chapters in this book, contributed by experienced members of first responder organisations or medical and research professionals, there is consistent affirmation of the importance of external support and the place of families. Whether it be individuals within the wider public that the first responder sees or the internal cultures that can affect their ability to remain happy and employed, external and family factors are the keys to ensuring each first responder can sustain a long and purposeful career.

To embrace the de-stigmatising conversations, programs and utilisation of partnership organisations, building a greater voice for mental fitness among the leaders of first responder agencies will be critical. The chapters in this book are testimony to the importance of leaders putting forward their experiences to highlight the positive impact that first responder roles can have. Leading, regardless of vocation, is demanding and difficult. Leading within a first responder agency takes on a new gravity, overseeing not just the operational requirements but also the physical and mental fitness of the leader's team. Supporting people's mental fitness as part of a team is a complex undertaking that is rarely taught to first responder leaders. With the complexity of our world rapidly increasing, the ability for first responder leaders to engage with mechanisms that can build the resilience of their first responder, and by extension their family, will be crucial to maintaining their mission which is to protect our health and wellbeing.

★ ★ ★ ★

Endnotes

1   *Answering the call*: Beyond Blue's National Mental a Health and Wellbeing Study of Police and Emergency Services, 2018, p.71.

2   *Answering the call,* p.71.

3   Sharp, M., et. al (2020). 'Assessing the mental health and wellbeing of the Emergency Responder.' King's College London, https://kcmhr.org/erreport2020-mentalhealth-wellbeing/.

4   Sharp, M., et. al (2020). 'Assessing the mental health and wellbeing of the Emergency Responder', p. 12.

5   Sharp, M., et. al (2020). 'Assessing the mental health and wellbeing of the Emergency Responder.' King's College London. https://kcmhr.org/erreport2020-mentalhealth-wellbeing/; p. 12.

6   Sharp, M., et. al (2020). 'Assessing the mental health and wellbeing of the Emergency Responder', p. 12.

7   McLennan,J. (2006). 'Survey of new volunteers at six months: April–September 2005 entry cohorts', Bushfire Cooperative Research Centre, School of Psychological Science, La Trobe University.

8   Dirkzwager, Anja & Bramsen, Inge & Ader, Herman & Ploeg, Henk. (2005). 'Secondary Traumatization in Partners and Parents of Dutch Peacekeeping Soldiers, in *Journal of Family Psychology*, Journal of the Division of Family Psychology of the American Psychological Association (Division 43). 19. 217–26. 10.1037/0893–3200.19.2.217.

9   Mikulincer, M et al. (1995). 'Martial intimacy, family support and secondary traumatization: A study of wives of veterans with combat stress reaction', *Anxiety and Coping* 8. pp. 203–13.

10 Galovski, T & Lyons, J. (2004). 'Psychological sequelae of combat violence: A review of the impact of PTSD on the veteran's family and possible interventions', *Aggression and Violent Behaviour* Volume 9, Issue 5, pp. 477–501.

11 van der Kolk, B. A. (1987). *Psychological trauma*. Washington: American Psychiatric Press.

12 Sharp, M., et. al (2020). 'Assessing the mental health and wellbeing of the Emergency Responder', p. 8.

13 Sharp, M., et. al (2020). 'Assessing the mental health and wellbeing of the Emergency Responder', p. 8.

14 Brough, P. (2004). 'Comparing the influence of traumatic and organizational stressors on the psychological health of police, fire, and ambulance officers, *International Journal of Stress Management*, 11, 227–44. doi: 10.1037/1072–5245.11.3.227.

15 Fullerton, C. (2004). 'Acute Stress Disorder, Posttraumatic Stress Disorder, and Depression in Disaster or Rescue Workers,' *American Journal of Psychiatry* 161(8):1370–6.

16 Corneil, W. (1999). 'Exposure to traumatic incidents and prevalence of posttraumatic stress symptomatology in urban firefighters in two countries' *Journal of Occupational Health Psychology*, 4, 131–141. doi: 10.1037/1076–8998.4.2.13.

17 Milligan-Saville, J et al. (2018). 'The Impact of Trauma Exposure on the Development of PTSD and Psychological Distress in a Volunteer Fire Service', *Psychiatry Research*, 270 (2018), 1110–15 <https://doi.org/10.1016/j.psychres.2018.06.058> p. 1110.

18 Stanley, I. H., Boffa, J. W., Hom, M. A., Kimbrel, N. A., Joiner, T. E., 2017. 'Differences in psychiatric symptoms and barriers to mental health care between volunteer and career firefighters', *Psychiatry Research*. pp. 247, 236–242.

19 Stanley, I. H., et al., *Psychiatry Research* pp. 247, 236–242.

20 'The people behind 000: mental health of our first responders' February 2019, Commonwealth of Australia 2019.

21 Royal Australian and New Zealand College of Psychiatrists, *Submission 15*, in 'The people behind 000: mental health of our first responders', February 2019 Commonwealth of Australia, 2019, p. 6, citations omitted.

22 Victoria Police Mental Health Strategy and Wellbeing Action Plan 2017–2020.

23 Corrigan, P and Watson, A. (2002) 'Understanding the impact of stigma on people with mental illness', in *World Journal of Psychiatry*, vol. 1, 2002, pp. 16–19.

24 Corrigan, P. 'How Stigma Interferes with Mental Health Care', *American Psychologist*, vol. 59, no. 7, 2004, pp. 614–25.

25 Hoge, C. et al. (2004). 'Combat Duty in Iraq and Afghanistan, Mental Health Problems, and Barriers to Care', *New England Journal of Medicine*, vol. 351, 2004, pp. 13–22; T. Britt, T. Greene-Shortridge and C. Castro, 'The Stigma of Mental Health Problems in the Military', *Military Medicine*, vol. 172, no. 2, 2007, pp. 157–61.

26 Corrigan, P and Watson, A. (2002). 'Understanding the impact of stigma on people with mental illness', in *World Journal of Psychiatry*, vol. 1, 2002, pp. 16–19.

27 Corrigan, P. 'How Stigma Interferes with Mental Health Care', in *American Psychologist*, vol. 59, no. 7, 2004, pp. 614–25.

28 K. Gallo, 'First person account: self-stigmatization', *Schizophr Bull*, vol. 20, 1994, pp. 407–08.

29 B. Link, E. Struening, S. Neese-Todd, S. Asmussen and J. Phelan, 'Stigma as a barrier to recovery: The consequences of stigma for the self-esteem of people with mental illnesses', *Psychiatric Services*, vol. 52, no. 12, 2001, pp. 1621–26.

30   *Australian Government Personnel Security Adjudicative Guidelines*, 2020.

31   *Australian Government Personnel Security Adjudicative Guidelines*, 2020.

32   https://www.ambulance.vic.gov.au/wp-content/uploads/2016/10/ambulance-victoria-mental-health-strategy-2016–19.pdf.

33   https://www.police.nsw.gov.au/__data/assets/pdf_file/0010/658513/NSWPF_2018-19_Annual_Report.pdf.

34   GB monthly report for claims up to April 2017 as cited in Victoria Police, ' Mental Health Strategy and Wellbeing Action Plan 2017–20'.

35   GB monthly report.

36   *The people behind 000: mental health of our first responders* (2019). Commonwealth of Australia 2019, https://www.aph.gov.au/Parliamentary_Business/Committees/Senate/Education_and_Employment/Mentalhealth/Report.

37   *Answering the call*, Beyond Blue's National Mental a Health and Wellbeing Study of Police and Emergency Services, 2018, p. 71.

38   J. Ozer, E. (2003) 'Predictors of Posttraumatic Stress Disorder and Symptoms in Adults: A Meta-Analysis', in Weiss, *Psychological Bulletin*, vol. 129, no. 1, 52–73.

39   Prati, G & Pietrantoni, L. (2009) 'Optimism, Social Support, and Coping Strategies As Factors Contributing to Posttraumatic Growth: A Meta-Analysis', *Journal of Loss and Trauma International Perspectives on Stress & Coping*, vol. 14, pp. 364–88.

40   Holt-Lundstad, J, Smith T. B., Layton J. B. (2010) Social Relationships and Mortality Risk: A Meta-analytic Review. PLoS Med 7(7): e1000316. https://doi.org/10.1371/journal.pmed.1000316.

41   GB monthly report.

42   Masi, Dale A. (2000): *Evaluating Your Employee Assistance and Managed Behavioral Care Program*, Washington, Dallen Inc, p. 13.

43   Phoenix Australia, AFP Structural Review, Reform and Policy Development on Mental Health: Final Report January 2018, p. 177.

44   Phoenix Australia, AFP Structural Review.

45   Phoenix Australia, AFP Structural Review.

46   Phoenix Australia, AFP Structural Review.

47   Phoenix Australia, AFP Structural Review.

48   **Recommendation 4**: The committee recommends that a Commonwealth-led process involving federal, state and territory governments be initiated to design and implement a national action plan on first responder mental health.

49   **Recommendation 10**: The committee recommends that the Commonwealth Government establish a national register of health professionals who specialise in first responder mental health..

50   Katy Kamkar and Konstantinos Papazoglou, 'Mitigating Risk Factors and Building Protective Factors as Prevention Strategies for Pubic Safely Personnel Duty Work'.

Further reading

Ambulance Victoria Mental Health and Wellbeing Strategy 2016–2019 https://www.ambulance.vic.gov.au/wp-content/uploads/2016/10/ambulance-victoria-mental-health-strategy-2016–19.pdf.

Answering the call: Beyond Blue's National Mental a Health and Wellbeing Study of Police and Emergency Services, 2018.

Australian Government Personnel Security Adjudicative Guidelines, 2020.

Britt, T. & Greene-Shortridge, T. & Castro, C. 'The Stigma of Mental Health Problems in the Military', *Military Medicine*, vol. 172, no. 2, 2007, pp. 157–61.

Brough, P. (2004). 'Comparing the influence of traumatic and organizational stressors on the psychological health of police, fire, and ambulance officers', *International Journal of Stress Management*, 11, 227–44. doi: 10.1037/1072–5245.11.3.227.

Corneil, W. (1999). 'Exposure to traumatic incidents and prevalence of posttraumatic stress symptomatology in urban firefighters in two countries', *Journal of Occupational Health Psychology*, 4, 131–141. doi: 10.1037/1076–8998.4.2.131.

Corrigan, P. 'How Stigma Interferes with Mental Health Care', *American Psychologist*, vol. 59, no. 7, 2004, pp. 614–25.

Corrigan, P. & Penn, D. (1999). 'Lessons from social psychology on discrediting psychiatric stigma', *American Psychologist*, vol. 54, 1999, pp. 765–76.

Corrigan, P & Watson, A. (2002). 'Understanding the impact of stigma on people with mental illness', *World Journal of Psychiatry*, vol. 1, 2002, pp. 16–19.

Dirkzwager, Anja & Bramsen, Inge & Ader, Herman & Ploeg, Henk. (2005). 'Secondary Traumatization in Partners and Parents of Dutch Peacekeeping Soldiers', *Journal of Family Psychology*: Journal of the Division of Family Psychology of the American Psychological Association (Division 43). 19. 217–26. 10.1037/0893–3200.19.2.217.

Ernst Kossek, E., & Ozeki, C. (1998). 'Work–family conflict, policies, and the job–life satisfaction relationship: A review and directions for organizational behavior–human resources research', *Journal of Applied Psychology*, vol. 83, no. 2, 139–149. https://doi.org/10.1037/0021–9010.83.2.139.

Fullerton, C. (2004)'Acute Stress Disorder, Posttraumatic Stress Disorder, and Depression in Disaster or Rescue Workers', *American Journal of Psychiatry*, vol. 161, no. 8, pp. 1370–76.

Gallo, K. (1994). 'First person account: self-stigmatization', *Schizophr Bull*, vol. 20, 1994, pp. 407–08.

Galovski, T & Lyons, J. (2004). 'Psychological sequelae of combat violence: a review of the impact of PTSD on the veteran's family and possible interventions' in *Aggression and Violent Behaviour*, vol. 9, issue 5, pp. 477–501.

Gibbs L, et. al. *Beyond Bushfires: Community Resilience and Recovery*, Final Report, November 2016, University of Melbourne.

Grzywacz, Joseph & Carlson, Dawn. (2007), 'Conceptualizing Work—Family Balance: Implications for Practice and Research', *Advances in Developing Human Resources*. 9. 455–471. 10.1177/1523422307305487.

Holt-Lunstad J, Smith T. B., Layton J. B. (2010), 'Social Relationships and Mortality Risk: A Meta-analytic Review', PLoS Med 7(7): e1000316. https://doi.org/10.1371/journal.pmed.1000316.

Hoge, C. et al. (2004). 'Combat Duty in Iraq and Afghanistan, Mental Health Problems, and Barriers to Care', *New England Journal of Medicine*, vol. 351, 2004, pp. 13–22.

Huizink, A. C. et. al (2006). 'Long term health complaints following the Amsterdam Air Disaster in police officers and fire-fighters', in *Occupational and environmental medicine, 63*(10), 657–662. https://doi.org/10.1136/oem.2005.024687.

Link, B. et al. (2001). 'Stigma as a barrier to recovery: The consequences of stigma for the self-esteem of people with mental illnesses', *Psychiatric Services*, vol. 52, no. 12, 2001, pp. 1621–26.

Masi, Dale A. (2000). Evaluating Your Employee Assistance and Managed Behavioural Care Program, (p. 13)—Washington: Dallen Inc.

McFarlane, A. (1990). 'An Australian Disaster: The 1983 Bushfires', *International Journal of Mental Health*, vol. 19, no. 2, Coping with Disasters: The Mental Health Component-2 (Summer 1990), pp. 36–47.

McLennan, J. (2006). 'Survey of new volunteers at six months: April–September 2005 entry cohorts', Bushfire Cooperative Research Centre, School of Psychological Science, La Trobe University.

Mikulincer, M et al. (1995). 'Marital intimacy, family support and secondary traumatization: A study of wives of veterans with combat stress reaction', *Anxiety and Coping*, no. 8, pp. 203–213.

Milligan-Saville, J et al. (2018). 'The Impact of Trauma Exposure on the Development of PTSD and Psychological Distress in a Volunteer Fire Service', *Psychiatry Research*, 270 (2018), 1110–15 <https://doi.org/10.1016/j.psychres.2018.06.058>.

NSW Police Force Annual Report 2018–2019 https://www.police.nsw.gov.au/__data/assets/pdf_file/0010/658513/NSWPF_2018-19_Annual_Report.pdf.

Ozer, E. (2003) 'Predictors of Posttraumatic Stress Disorder and Symptoms in Adults: A Meta-Analysis', *Weiss Psychological Bulletin*, vol. 129, no. 1, pp. 52–73.

Pearrow, M. & Cosgrove, L. (2009). 'The Aftermath of Combat-Related PTSD: Toward an Understanding of Transgenerational Trauma', *Communication Disorders Quarterly*, 30. 10.1177/1525740108328227.

Phoenix Australia, 'AFP Structural Review, Reform and Policy Development on Mental Health', Final Report, January 2018.

Prati, G & Pietrantoni, L. (2009) 'Optimism, Social Support, and Coping Strategies As Factors Contributing to Posttraumatic Growth: A Meta-Analysis', in *Journal of Loss and Trauma* , International Perspectives on Stress and Coping, vol. 14, pp. 364–88.

Rebekah M. Doley, R. et al. (2016) 'An Investigation Into the Relationship Between Long-term Posttraumatic Stress Disorder Symptoms and Coping in Australian Volunteer Firefighters', *Journal of Nervous and Mental Disease*, vol. 204, no. 7.

Royal Australian and New Zealand College of Psychiatrists, *Submission 15*, 'The people behind 000: mental health of our first responders', February 2019, Commonwealth of Australia 2019, p. 6, citations omitted.

Rutter, M. (1985). 'Resilience in the face of adversity: Protective factors and resistance to psychiatric disorder', *British Journal of Psychiatry, 147*, 598–611. https://doi.org/10.1192/bjp.147.6.598.

Sharp, M., et al. (2020). 'Assessing the mental health and wellbeing of the Emergency Responders', King's College London https://kcmhr.org/erreport2020-mentalhealth-wellbeing/.

Stanley, I. H., Boffa, J. W., Hom, M. A., Kimbrel, N. A., Joiner, T. E., 2017, 'Differences in psychiatric symptoms and barriers to mental health care between volunteer and career firefighters', *Psychiatry Research*, no. 247, pp. 236–242.

The people behind 000: mental health of our first responders (2019). Commonwealth of Australia 2019, https://www.aph.gov.au/Parliamentary_Business/Committees/Senate/Education_and_Employment/Mentalhealth/Report.

van der Kolk, B. A. (1987), *Psychological trauma*. Washington, American Psychiatric Press.

Victoria Police, Mental Health Strategy and Wellbeing Action Plan 2017–2020.

Voydanoff, P. (2005) 'Toward a Conceptualization of Perceived Work-Family Fit and Balance: A Demands and Resources Approach', *Journal of Marriage and Family*, https://doi.org/10.1111/j.1741–3737.2005.00178.x.

Yuan, C. et al. (2011). 'Protective factors for posttraumatic stress disorder symptoms in a prospective study of police officers' *Psychiatry Research*, vol. 188, no. 1, pp 45–50. https://doi.org/10.1016/j.psychres.2010.10.034.

Postscript

Tom Frame

Several of the contributors to this book have referred to moral injury in their account of vocational wellbeing. It is essentially a new term for an old experience. The concept of moral injury can be explained with the help of a universal human experience. We have all sustained physical injuries that have affected our ability to function. We take these kinds of injuries for granted. They happen; they are part of life. We engage in behaviour knowing we might get hurt and we realise that, from time to time, someone else's actions might result in us being harmed. Some injuries might lead to permanent disability; some injuries produce temporary inability; some injuries cause pain but have no other lasting affect. But can we be *morally* injured?

The notion of moral injury was first proposed by the American psychologist Jonathan Shay after years of working with veterans of the Vietnam War. Shay thought that moral injury was present when 'there has been a betrayal of what is morally correct; by someone who holds legitimate authority; and, in a high-stakes situation'. Brett Litz, another American psychologist, expanded Shay's definition to include 'maladaptive beliefs about the self and the world' in response to 'perpetrating, bearing witness to, failing to prevent, or learning about acts that transgress deeply held moral beliefs and expectations'. Moral injury is portrayed as an unseen wound to the inner self. This wound is hard to describe—it cannot be seen—but its consequences are manifest in conduct. It has also been argued that collective moral injury is a possibility when a whole nation is injured by the moral failings of its leaders, failings that damage and debilitate the common life of the body politic.

For me, the definitions offered by Shay and Litz prompt more questions than they disclose answers. What is actually *injured in a moral injury*? Is it an affliction of the psyche or the conscience or the reason? It is damage to that part of the brain responsible for moral thought or does it disturb a person's essential being more broadly? Is a moral injury different from an ethical injury, or synonymous with it? Is the injury self-inflicted, inflicted by others, or the unavoidable outcome of particular circumstances? Are certain groups more susceptible to moral injury than others depending on their age, gender, ethnicity or culture? Does a strong religious faith, or a well-developed moral code, offer protection against incurring a moral injury? Is moral injury inflicted instantaneously from a particular experience or is it sustained gradually from reflection on a series of events? Does the injury cause permanent damage or lead to short-term debilitation only? Does an individual recognise they could be, or have been, morally injured and how this could realisation affect both their being and their behaviour?

If we accept the possibility of moral injury, there may be an infinite number of ways for a person to be morally injured depending on personality and circumstances.

Plainly, a great many questions can be posed of the conceptual dimensions of moral injury before we even start to address its practical dimensions. Although research into the experience has barely begun in the United States, and is practically non-existent in Australia, the term moral injury has nonetheless gained currency in the popular press and in scholarly journals both here and abroad. An uninformed reader could be excused for thinking that the existence of 'moral injury' was undisputed; its meaning uncontested; and the underpinning research highly textured. Despite 'moral injury' being applied to a number of unseen or non-visible wounds sustained principally in the context of armed conflict (such as those sustained by soldiers, police, aid workers and diplomats), many of the definitions are vague or unclear, suggestive more than specific, short on detail and lacking empirical substantiation. Most definitions fail to identify the part of the person affected by moral injury or explain why an experience is morally injurious. Going back to our shared experience: physical injuries can be observed and addressed because they are consistent in form and comparable in character; in contrast moral injuries cannot be seen and they affect people differently. Moral injury is heavily dependent on a person's experiences of the world and its operation, their personal values and virtues and the way they interpret what they see and hear.

To date, inquiries into the incidence, prevalence and severity of moral injury have focussed on the military community although researchers agree it is not restricted to uniformed personnel. At least in theory, individuals employed in most professions could sustain a moral injury. For instance, people working in the medical profession could be morally injured by the requirement to make unpalatable decisions about the quality of patient care when hospital resources are limited. Veterinarians could be morally injured by requests to destroy perfectly healthy dogs because greyhound racing has been banned. Police could be morally injured by political direction to focus on trivial crimes attracting media attention when serious crimes are largely ignored. Those in the legal profession can be morally injured by plea-bargaining or by perceived inequities in sentencing guidelines. All professions try to avoid the possibility of their members suffering something resembling a moral injury by the imposition of codes of conduct, although many confuse morality with legality, and they may or may not be an effective preventative measure. They don't hurt but do they help? Plainly, any and every human occupation is associated with moral questions and ethical dilemmas that often oblige the individual to make painful choices between the lesser of two evils. Such situations force people to act in a manner that is morally perplexing but does it *injure* them?

We might also imagine that the experience of moral injury varies with host nation and popular culture. Inasmuch as morals embody and reflect culture, the causes and the consequences of moral injury will be shaped by the general and specific cultures refracted through national identity that shape the individual moral self and prepare them to negotiate moral dilemmas. Some cultures, for example, appear to place a lesser value on human life or give less emphasis to social equality. Negotiating these differences could be devastating for an outsider.

The character of moral injury is also likely to vary with the passage of time and with seasons of life. As social norms and cultural conventions change rapidly in Western societies, shifts in historic attitudes will bear directly on the likelihood and the severity of moral injury. We look back on slavery and imperialism with horror although neither were seen as especially egregious at many points in human history. And because the moral self develops and matures with the ebb and flow of life, whatever constitutes an offence against the beliefs that undergird the moral self (whether it is denial, betrayal or contravention of those beliefs) will reflect shifts in social attitudes and personal opinions. In old age I might abhor behaviour I applauded in my youth.

I formed a small project team at UNSW Canberra in 2015 to consider the whole notion of unseen wounds and how they might be differentiated from post-traumatic stress disorder. After months of deliberation and debate, we defined moral injury as: 'the result of harm or damage (which leaves a wound) that reduces the functioning or impairs the performance of the moral self (which causes an injury), which is that part of a person where moral reasoning and moral decision-making takes place.' We concluded that exposure to, or participation in, actions that violate an individual's own moral code cause moral injury. Why? Because they destabilise the moral norms an individual uses to makes sense of themselves and the world. Moral injury can be sustained through acts of commission and omission. The extent to which these moral norms are ignored, denied or betrayed determine the severity of the injury, along with the strength of the beliefs and their nature—whether they are foundational, supportive or expressive—within the moral self.

A person can simultaneously incur a moral injury and suffer PTSD through a single event or experience. Let me make this foundational observation: trauma needs to be present in a diagnosis of PTSD. It is not required in the case of moral injury. For a person to be morally injured their moral values, their moral reasoning and their moral compass must be affected in some way. The involvement of morality makes moral injury different from PTSD and other occupation-related mental health conditions and psychological disorders.

We then asked: what are the moral values and virtues that are most likely to be injured. Drawing on personal testimonies and a range of anecdotal evidence, we identified a willingness to trust, a readiness to show loyalty, adherence to conviction and confidence in judgement as being among the individual moral values and virtues most affected by moral injury.

The next task was outlining any specifically Australian characteristics of moral injury. After all, we are not Americans and our popular culture is unique. We discerned that Australians are generally more unsettled by how things are done and less with why things are done. We are not a people given to abstraction and we prefer to disengage from politics and arguments about theories or ideologies. We are usually preoccupied with pragmatic issues and less with principles—although any violation of values and virtues during the conduct of an activity (and these involve practical principles) often leads to moral injury—and someone deciding they are moral and colleagues or the organisation are immoral. Although most researchers agree that moral values are shaped by culture and each nation has its own distinctive cultural traits, it is not yet possible to determine any specifically Australian characteristics of moral injury beyond these very general observations.

Having come to this subject of moral injury with an open-mind, we then reviewed the existing literature. Most accounts of moral injury have been offered by psychologists drawing on ideas and insights that were, in fact, originally the focus of philosophical inquiry. Much of the language used in these accounts lacks precision and an awareness of the nuances and subtleties associated with concepts like guilt and shame, remorse and regret, forgiveness and absolution. These are not psychological terms, they are philosophical ones. They are not parts of personality that belong to workplace specialists, they animate the workforce and they are of critical interest to leaders. This lack of precision has contributed to the difficulties associated with differentiating moral injury from PTSD and for the depiction of moral injury as a 'mental health issue' rather than an unavoidable feature of working in any organisation that intertwines personal identity and corporate narrative. By this I mean we ask employees to absorb, own and even live the company story. People become police, firefighters, ambulance paramedics. It is not just what they do; it is who they are. We suggested that where moral injury is not coincident with PTSD it should be considered an existential condition needing to be addressed rather than being deemed a disorder that ought to be treated. Future research into moral injury ought, therefore, to concentrate on the moral character of the events which are thought to cause injury and focus specifically on how moral injury impairs individual performance. Such research would assist leaders in determining the moral fitness of their followers, negotiating the moral complexity of their assigned tasks, and ensuring their moral health as part of a holistic regard for each person for whom the leader has accepted responsibility.

We concluded that moral injury can be experienced in five different ways. *First*, it is a form of *disturbance* producing a crisis in moral beliefs and prompting confusion about the world's moral reliability. Moral injury is associated with a rupture in the relationship between the moral culture in which an individual is raised and their experience beyond that nurturing culture. Moral injury is, therefore, context and time specific. A person interprets an experience of moral injury in relation to their specific circumstances and values at that point in life. In another place or at another time, that person might not be morally injured by the same experience or a similar one. Understood in this way, moral injury is not a sign of mental illness or a psychological disorder, but a collapse of personal meaning and individual identity. The world appears to be bereft of order and lack coherence.

Second, moral injury is a form of *alienation* that occurs when an individual believes they are responsible and culpable, in whole or in part, for an act they regard as morally impermissible and which they cannot assimilate, integrate or accommodate into their pre-existing systems of meaning. Moral injury is, in this sense, a self-inflicted violation of one's own moral conscience producing profound feelings of guilt. In contrast to moral *injury*, individuals experience moral *affront* when confronted by, or the subject of, an act they regard as morally intolerable. The processes of reconciliation and forgiveness will differ depending on whether the individual believes they are to blame or places the blame elsewhere.

Third, moral injury can be also portrayed as a *violation* of an individual's moral conscience following an act of perceived moral transgression that produces profound emotional shame or anguish. This definition presumes that a person can be morally injured only if they possess deeply held and clearly articulated ethical beliefs about right and wrong. A morally injurious experience is one that transgresses these beliefs and clear or continuing contravention of these beliefs (by themselves or others) can cause moral injury. The moral individual who witnesses what they consider wrongdoing but does nothing to prevent its continuation is injured by their inactivity. They become party (or an accessory) to the act because they do not protest against it or report it and making themselves complicit in the act, means the moral injury is a self-inflicted wound. A profound sense of shame, guilt or anguish characterises these injuries.

Fourth, moral injury can be understood as a form of *damage* which impairs the functioning of a person's moral health and wellbeing. A person who witnesses the commission or the consequences of wrongdoing may internalise an experience so that it traduces their own ability to think and act morally. Their exposure to moral evil might change their behaviour including becoming cynical about human nature, lacking sympathy for others, being unable to empathise with others, being hasty in criticising others and displaying greater tolerance for the alleged immorality of others. They may also reject the existence of universal moral values; feel guilt for acting wrongly or not acting rightly; and, believe in their guilt even if the action in question is justified in the eyes of others. Moral injury is essentially a damaged moral self.

Fifth, moral injury is associated with the *disorientation* of a person's moral compass when their worldview is shattered after observing or participating in actions they deem to be immoral. The disorientation leads the person to question the validity and necessity of moral values; lament the discontinuities between the idealised moral self and the realised self; and, resist claims that the world conveys a universal moral logic. For such disorientation, observing cruelty and callousness is enough; it does not matter whether the person did something or nothing. The observation itself undermines the person's convictions about what constitutes moral behaviour. The extent of the disorientation depends on the strength of their moral convictions and the nature and duration of their exposure to immoral acts. The disorientation may lead the person to rationalise immoral acts and normalise criminal acts.

Each of these five experiences suggest that moral injury is sustained by participation and observation of something the observer deems to be immoral. The interpretation of the event appears to be crucial to whether a person sustains a wound and the nature of the injury that results. The interpretative process is highly subjective influenced as it is by diverse personal beliefs, convictions and values. Thus, two people could observe the same action and come to contradictory conclusions about its moral status. But while consensus exists on what might cause moral injury, these competing accounts differ as to its consequences. Some approaches see the injury confined to a person's inner being; others find it manifested in conduct. The connection between cause and effect, and between being and behaving, is yet to be the subject of close attention in accounts of moral injury.

Our inquiries lead us to believe there are probably three main consequences associated with moral injury, consequences that need to be validated by research. The *first* is that moral injury has a bearing on personal wholeness and wellbeing. Individuals are morally injured—part of them is damaged—and their wounds need attention. *Second*, the morally injured do not function with the same moral agility or consistency as they did before being wounded. *Third*, the morally injured have wounds that affect their personal and professional interactions. For instance, their injuries might have depleted their ability to trust other people, damaged their confidence in institutional leadership and disrupted their confidence in moral principles. These affected interactions have a bearing on their public duties, their attitude to the profession of which they are members and their regard for the state. There may be other causes and consequences of moral injury too. But we believe that we have gained a sense of the origins of moral injury, observed its main features and discerned its enduring outcomes.

The message from the contributors to this book is consistent: moral injury has a direct bearing on the vocational wellbeing of first responders. When no-one is encouraged to pursue moral excellence; when colleagues or supervisors engage regularly in immoral conduct; when such misconduct is not reported and left unchastened; when influential people become indifferent to exemplary moral leadership; when moral standards are eroded by a steadily self-interested culture; when pragmatism is esteemed over principle; when only objectives and outcomes matter; when a person's worth is determined by their practical utility rather than their human dignity; the incidence of moral injury is greatly magnified and its severity is likely to increase.

Vocations are set apart by moral codes that bind members to shared values that impart identity and disclose destiny. If the unifying moral code is abandoned, a sense of vocation is lost and a job is all that remains. Vocational covenants that spoke of privileges and responsibilities are replaced with contracts that disclose only duties and obligations. For those who feel called to the vocation of a first responder, their sense of wellbeing is inevitably undermined by waning trust and implicit suspicion in the form of more intrusive oversight and more draconian compliance regimes. The positive benefits of serving are diminished and the community is impoverished as first responders are reduced to mere functionaries—doing no more than they are paid to do. For those enduring some form of traumatic stress or battling the onset of burn-out from unrelenting pressure, losing their vocation will further deplete their wellbeing and inevitably produce a personal crisis that may take considerable time to resolve. In such circumstances, the first responder will need extensive respite and perhaps a new direction in life.

When someone decides they are unable to serve as a first responder with moral integrity, the cause is more than a personal malaise because the problem is no longer limited to an individual. In most cases, the organisational culture has been found wanting and a collective failure of leadership has occurred. Declining culture and defective leadership often start imperceptibly with poor practices and bad decisions. Attentiveness to human need—an essential element of moral leadership—ensures the slide into deviancy and decadence can be reversed. The contributors to this collection have, in their own ways, made an appeal for closer consideration of human nature and invited a more compassionate response to human frailty. When we ponder what most first responders are obliged to endure as part of their service, anything other than the exercise of generous care seems counter-productive and mean-spirited. This is perhaps the most important message to be drawn from reflecting on the perspectives on first responder service offered in this book.

www.ingramcontent.com/pod-product-compliance
Lightning Source LLC
Chambersburg PA
CBHW041934260326

41914CB00010B/1294